WHEN THE CHRIST CAME

THE ROAD
TO JERUSALEM

The Bible for School and Home

by J. Paterson Smyth

The Book of Genesis

Moses and the Exodus

Joshua and the Judges

The Prophets and Kings

When the Christ Came:
The Highlands of Galilee

When the Christ Came:
The Road to Jerusalem

St. Matthew

St. Mark

WHEN THE CHRIST CAME

THE ROAD
TO JERUSALEM

by

J. Paterson Smyth

YESTERDAY'S CLASSICS

ITHACA, NEW YORK

This edition, first published in 2017 by Yesterday's Classics, an imprint of Yesterday's Classics, LLC, is an unabridged republication of the text originally published by Sampson Low, Marston & Co., Ltd. For the complete listing of the books that are published by Yesterday's Classics, please visit www.yesterdaysclassics. com. Yesterday's Classics is the publishing arm of the Baldwin Online Children's Literature Project which presents the complete text of hundreds of classic books for children at www.mainlesson.com.

ISBN: 978-1-63334-033-6

Yesterday's Classics, LLC
PO Box 339
Ithaca, NY 14851

CONTENTS

CONTENTS

GENERAL INTRODUCTION

I

This series of books is intended for two classes of teachers:

1. *For Teachers in Week Day and Sunday Schools.* For these each book is divided into complete lessons. The lesson will demand preparation. Where feasible there should be diligent use of commentaries and of any books indicated in the notes. *As a general rule* I think the teacher should not bring the book at all to his class if he is capable of doing without it. He should make copious notes of the subject. The lesson should be thoroughly studied and digested beforehand, with all the additional aids at his disposal, and it should come forth at the class warm and fresh from his own heart and brain. But I would lay down no rigid rule about the use of the Lesson Book. To some it may be a burden to keep the details of a long lesson in the memory; and, provided the subject has been very carefully studied, the Lesson Book, with its salient points carefully marked in coloured pencil, may be a considerable help. Let each do what seems best in his particular case, only taking care to satisfy his conscience that it is not done through

1

laziness, and that he can really do best for his class by the plan which he adopts.

2. *For Parents* who would use it in teaching their children at home. They need only small portions, brief little lessons of about ten minutes each night. For these each chapter is divided into short sections. I should advise that on the first night only the Scripture indicated should be read, with some passing remarks and questions to give a grip of the story. That is enough. Then night after night go on with the teaching, taking as much or as little as one sees fit.

I have not written out the teaching in full as a series of readings which could be read over to the child without effort or thought. With this book in hand a very little preparation and adaptation will enable one to make the lesson more interesting and more personal and to hold the child's attention by questioning. Try to get his interest. Try to make him talk. Make the lesson conversational. Don't preach.

II

HINTS FOR TEACHING

An ancient Roman orator once laid down for his pupils the three-fold aim of a teacher:

1. *Placere* (to interest).

2. *Docere* (to teach).

3. *Movere* (to move).

1. To interest the audience (in order to teach them).

2. To teach them (in order to move them).

3. To move them to action.

On these three words of his I hang a few suggestions on the teaching of this set of Lessons.

1. *Placere (to interest)*

I want especially to insist on attention to this rule. Some teachers seem to think that to interest the pupils is a minor matter. It is not a minor matter and the pupils will very soon let you know it. Believe me, it is no waste of time to spend hours during the week in planning to excite their interest to the utmost. Most of the complaints of inattention would cease at once if the teacher would give more study to rousing their interest. After all, there is little use in knowing the facts of your subject, and being anxious about the souls of the pupils, if all the time that you are teaching, these pupils are yawning and taking no interest in what you say. I know some have more aptitude for teaching than others. Yet, after considerable experience of teachers whose lesson was a weariness to the flesh, and of teachers who never lost attention for a moment, I am convinced, on the whole, that the power to interest largely depends on the previous preparation.

Therefore do not content yourself with merely studying the teaching of this series. Read widely and freely. Read not only commentaries, but books that will give local interest and colour—books that will throw valuable sidelights on your sketch.

But more than reading is necessary. You know the meaning of the expression, *"Put yourself in his place."* Practise that in every Bible story, using your imagination, living in the scene, experiencing, as far as you can, every feeling of the actors. To some this is no effort at all. They feel their cheeks flushing and their eyes growing moist as they project themselves involuntarily into the scene before them. But though it be easier to some than to others, it is in some degree possible to all, and the interest of the lesson largely depends on it. I have done my best in these books to help the teacher in this respect. But no man can help another much. Success will depend entirely on the effort to "put yourself in his place."

In reading the Bible chapter corresponding to each lesson, I suggest that the teacher should read part of the chapter, rather than let the pupils tire themselves by "reading round." My experience is that this "reading round" is a fruitful source of listlessness. When his verse is read, the pupil can let his mind wander till his turn comes again, and so he loses all interest. I have tried, with success, varying the monotony. I would let them read the first round of verses in order; then I would make them read out of the regular order, as I called their names; and sometimes, if the lesson were long, I would again and again interrupt by reading a group of verses myself, making remarks as I went on. To lose their interest is fatal.

I have indicated also in the lessons that you should not unnecessarily give information yourself. Try to question it *into* them. If you tell them facts which they have just read, they grow weary. If you ask a question, and then answer it yourself when they miss it, you cannot keep their attention. Send your questions around in every sort of order, or want of order. Try to puzzle them—try to surprise them. Vary the form of the question, if not answered, and always feel it to be a defeat if you ultimately fail in getting the answer you want.

2. *Docere (to teach)*

You interest the pupil in order that you may *teach.* Therefore teach definitely the Lesson that is set you. Do not be content with interesting him. Do not be content either with drawing spiritual teaching. Teach the facts before you. Be sure that God has inspired the narration of them for some good purpose.

When you are dealing with Old Testament characters, do not try to shirk or to condone evil in them. They were not faultless saints. They were men like ourselves, whom God was helping and bearing with, as He helps and bears with us, and the interest of the story largely depends on the pupil realizing this.

In the Old Testament books of this series you will find very full chapters written on the Creation, the Fall, the Flood, the election of Jacob, the Sun standing still, the slaughter of Canaanites, and other such subjects. In connection with these I want to say something that especially concerns teachers. Your pupils, now or later, can hardly avoid coming in contact with the flippant scepticism so common nowadays, which makes jests at the story of the sun standing still, and talks of the folly of believing that all humanity was condemned because Eve ate an apple thousands of years ago. This flippant tone is "in the air." They will meet with it in their companions, in the novels of the day, in popular magazine articles on their tables at home. You have, many of you, met with it yourselves; you know how disturbing it is; and you probably know, too, that much of its influence on people arises from the narrow and unwise teaching of the Bible in their youth. Now you have no right to ignore this in your teaching of the Bible. You need not talk of Bible difficulties and their answers. You need not refer to them at all. But teach the truth that will take the sting out of these difficulties when presented in after-life.

To do this requires trouble and thought. We have learned much in the last fifty years that has thrown new light for us on the meaning of some parts of the Bible; which has, at any rate, made doubtful some of our old interpretations of it. We must not ignore this. There are certain traditional theories which some of us still insist on teaching as God's infallible truth, whereas they are really only human opinions about it, which may possibly be mistaken. As long as they are taught as human opinions, even if we are wrong, the mistake will do no harm. But if things are taught as God's infallible truth, to be believed on peril of doubting God's Word, it may do grave mischief, if in after-life the pupil find them seriously disputed, or perhaps false. A shallow, unthinking man, finding part of his teaching false, which has been associated in his mind with the most solemn sanctions of religion, is in danger of letting the whole go. Thus many of our young people drift into hazy doubt about the Bible. Then we get troubled about their beliefs, and give them books of Christian evidences to win them back by explaining that what was taught them in childhood was not *quite* correct, and needs now to be modified by a broader and slightly different view. But we go on as before with the younger generation, and expose them in their turn to the same difficulties.

Does it not strike you that, instead of this continual planning to win men back from unbelief, it might be worth while to try the other method of not exposing them to unbelief? Give them the more careful and intelligent teaching at first, and so prepare them to meet the difficulties by-and-by.

I have no wish to advocate any so-called "advanced" teaching. Much of such teaching I gravely object to. But there are truths of which there is no question amongst thoughtful people, which somehow are very seldom taught to the young, though ignorance about them in after-life leads to grave doubt and misunderstanding. Take, for example, the gradual, progressive nature of God's teaching in Scripture, which makes the Old Testament teaching as a whole lower than that of the New. This is certainly no doubtful question, and the knowledge of it is necessary for an intelligent study of

Scripture. I have dealt with it where necessary in some of the books of this series.

I think, too, our teaching on what may seem to us doubtful questions should be more fearless and candid. If there are two different views each held by able and devout men, do not teach your own as the infallibly true one, and ignore or condemn the other. For example, do not insist that the order of creation must be accurately given in the first chapter of Genesis. You may think so; but many great scholars, with as deep a reverence for the Bible as you have, think that inspired writers were circumscribed by the science of their time. Do not be too positive that the story of the Fall *must be* an exactly literal narrative of facts. If you believe that it is I suppose you must tell your pupil so. But do not be afraid to tell him also that there are good and holy and scholarly men who think of it as a great old-world allegory, like the parable of the Prodigal Son, to teach in easy popular form profound lessons about sin. Endeavor in your Bible teaching "to be thoroughly truthful: to assert nothing as certain which is not certain, nothing as probable which is not probable, and nothing as more probable than it is." Let the pupil see that there are some things that we cannot be quite sure about, and let him gather insensibly from your teaching the conviction that truth, above all things, is to be loved and sought, and that religion has never anything to fear from discovering the truth. If we could but get this healthy, manly, common-sense attitude adopted now in teaching the Bible to young people, we should, with

GENERAL INTRODUCTION

God's blessing, have in the new generation a stronger and more intelligent faith.

3. *Movere (to move)*

All your teaching is useless unless it have this object: to move the heart, to rouse the affections toward the love of God, and the will toward the effort after the blessed life. You interest in order to teach. You teach in order to move. *That* is the supreme object. Here the teacher must be left largely to his own resources. One suggestion I offer: don't preach. At any rate, don't preach much lest you lose grip of your pupils. You have their attention all right while their minds are occupied by a carefully prepared lesson; but wait till you close your Bible, and, assuming a long face, begin, "And now, boys," etc. and straightway they know what is coming, and you have lost them in a moment.

Do not change your tone at the application of your lesson. Try to keep the teaching still conversational. Try still in this more spiritual part of your teaching to question into them what you want them to learn. Appeal to the judgment and to the conscience. I can scarce give a better example than that of our Lord in teaching the parable of the Good Samaritan. He first interested His pupil by putting His lesson in an attractive form, and then He did not append to it a long, tedious moral. He simply asked the man before Him, "Which of these three *thinkest thou?*"—i.e., "What do you think about it?" The interest was still kept up. The man, pleased at the appeal to his judgment, replied promptly, "He that showed mercy on him;" and on the instant came the quick rejoinder, "Go, and do thou likewise." Thus the lesson ends. Try to work on that model.

Now, while forbidding preaching to your pupils, may I be permitted a little preaching myself? This series of lessons is intended for Sunday schools as well as week-day schools. It is of Sunday-school teachers I am thinking in what I am now about to say. I cannot escape the solemn feeling of the responsibility of every teacher for the children in his care. Some of these children have little or no religious influence exerted on them for the whole week except in this one hour with you. Do not make light of this work. Do not get to think, with good-natured optimism, that all the nice, pleasant children in your class are pretty sure to be Christ's soldiers and servants by-and-by. Alas! for the crowds of these nice, pleasant children, who, in later life, wander away from Christ into the ranks of evil. Do not take this danger lightly. Be anxious; be prayerful; be terribly in earnest, that the one hour in the week given you to use be wisely and faithfully used.

But, on the other hand, be very hopeful too, because of the love of God. He will not judge you hardly. Remember that He will bless very feeble work, if it be your best. Remember that He cares infinitely more for the children's welfare than you do, and, therefore, by His grace, much of the teaching about which you are despondent may bring forth good fruit in the days to come. Do you know the lines about "The Noisy Seven"?—

"I wonder if he remembers—
    Our sainted teacher in heaven—
The class in the old grey schoolhouse,
    Known as the 'Noisy Seven'?

"I wonder if he remembers
    How restless we used to be.
Or thinks we forget the lesson
    Of Christ and Gethsemane?

"I wish I could tell the story
    As he used to tell it then;
I'm sure that, with Heaven's blessing,
    It would reach the hearts of men.

"I often wish I could tell him,
    Though we caused him so much pain
By our thoughtless, boyish frolic,
    His lessons were not in vain.

"I'd like to tell him how Willie,
    The merriest of us all,
From the field of Balaclava
    Went home at the Master's call.

"I'd like to tell him how Ronald,
    So brimming with mirth and fun,
Now tells the heathen of India
    The tale of the Crucified One.

"I'd like to tell him how Robert,
    And Jamie, and George, and 'Ray,'
Are honoured in the Church of God—
    The foremost men of their day.

"I'd like, yes, I'd like to tell him
    What his lesson did for me;
And how I am trying to follow
    The Christ of Gethsemane.

"Perhaps he knows it already,
    For Willie has told him, maybe,
That we are all coming, coming
    Through Christ of Gethsemane.

"How many besides I know not
    Will gather at last in heaven,
The fruit of that faithful sowing,
    But the sheaves are already seven."

INTRODUCTORY

LESSON I

A HARVEST FESTIVAL IN JERUSALEM

St. John VII. 14-18 and 25-52.

Do not read this Scripture at beginning. Wait for its right place after introductory matter and trace on map the journey from Capernaum to Jerusalem.

Point out first that our Lord's public life divides itself into two parts:

1. The Public Ministry in Galilee,

2. Going up to Jerusalem to die,

and that the first of these has been dealt with in the previous lessons. Now open all Bibles and look at St. Luke ix. 51 and make all pupils repeat this important verse:

Now when the time was well nigh come that He should be received up, He steadfastly set His face to go to Jerusalem.

15

§ 1. *How St. Luke Wrote His Gospel*

We are now beginning second part of the Lord's life. What writer has written this verse? St. Luke. Now put a mark in every Bible at this verse. Then let pupils turn over to xviii. 14, and hold this intervening sheaf of pages separate. This is a new section which St. Luke has inserted in the Gospel. It is mainly the memories of the Road to Jerusalem which he had gathered from old disciples and friends who had been with Jesus thirty years before. And this verse just read contains the opening words.

How St. Luke wrote his Gospel is an interesting story. We find him in the Acts and St. Paul's Epistles—a young physician of literary instincts, travelling about with St. Paul. He carried with him in his baggage two manuscript books. One was a Diary, which was afterwards to be published as a Life of St. Paul in the Acts of the Apostles; the other, to be published first, was his chief book. He had set his heart on writing a Life of our Lord fuller than the other Gospels and Paul was helping him. As he moved about he was continually meeting old disciples who had been with Jesus thirty years ago and who remembered many things not already written. Think of his delight the day he heard the lovely story of The Prodigal Son—or when he heard, perhaps from the Blessed Virgin herself in Jerusalem, the story of "when shepherds watched their flocks by night." How he would hurry back to write them down. This whole section (chaps. ix. to xviii.) was mainly concerned with the Road to Jerusalem.

§ 2. The Two Stories

Now when Jesus bade good-bye to Galilee, He was going up to the Harvest Festival (the Feast of Tabernacles), one of the great annual feasts, where He would find a million of Jews from all over the world, assembled in Jerusalem, a splendid opportunity for teaching about His Kingdom. But the Jews would not listen. They turned Him out every time He got in, and tried to kill Him. So He had to go and teach outside in the roads and villages where He could and wait to get in again at the next Festival. That is why the whole story up to the Crucifixion is about six months long. It was a hard time, travelling in the winter and always in danger.

Long after another disciple, St. John, wrote his memories of this time. Curiously he only tells each time of what happened *in* Jerusalem, while St. Luke only tells of what happened *outside* Jerusalem on the road. It is like two stories of the Siege of Paris in 1870, where one writer was inside and couldn't get out, and the other writer was outside and couldn't get in. We have to combine the town story of St. John with the country story of St. Luke to find what happened.

§ 3. Harvest Festival in Jerusalem

Now we resume the narrative. He left Galilee and travelled towards Jerusalem. The Samaritans stopped Him (St. Luke ix. 52) and He had to change His route. After a while He got to Bethany, four miles out of Jerusalem. There He was received in the house of

17

Lazarus and Martha and Mary, who afterwards became His very close friends. Do you remember the wonderful things that happened about Lazarus six months later? There He slept that night, while right across the valley were the lights of Jerusalem and the vast assembled crowds. Next day He made His entrance. Therefore we must leave St. Luke's country story and go to St. John's town story.

Here read St. John vii. 14-18 and 25-32.

Now it is the 18th of October, A.D. 28. (The month Tisri). The Feast of Tabernacles, the Harvest Festival, is in full swing, the brightest, gladdest holiday of all the year. The Feast of a nation resting from its work. "The Feast of Ingathering at the end of the year when thou hast gathered in thy labours out of the field." Everybody went to this popular festival. It was a joyous, dramatic representation of the old Wilderness days when their fathers dwelt in tents. People lived in the open air in booths of green branches of olive and vine with bunches of ripe fruit hanging over the booths. There they kept holiday. The old Rabbis used to say, "He who has not seen this Festival does not know what joy means."

§ 4. Nicodemus and the Police

The Festival was half over when Jesus appeared. There had been much disappointment, for He was already famous and the strangers all wanted to see and hear Him. Unexpectedly they came on Him teaching in the Temple. What first surprised them as they listened? (*v.* 15). What did Jesus reply? "If any man willeth," etc.

What did that mean? Think. Yes. To know God is not a mere matter of brains. It is the Heart and the Will more than the intellect that finds God. He that willeth to do God's will he shall know. So a very clever man may miss Him, while a poor ignorant man finds Him. That is the encouragement for plain, simple people.

Now as He goes out, St. John hears the muttered talk. They are wondering why the rulers do not arrest Him. "Is not this He," etc. (*vv.* 25-27). "Is it because they know He is the very Christ?" Was it? Ah! no. Why did they not stop Him? They dared not lay hands on Him with that sympathetic multitude around. As we saw already, the common people were on His side. And the crowd of foreign Jews were not afraid of the priests like the Jerusalem Jews. So the rulers were afraid. But they could not stand it when they heard the multitude speaking in His favour and believing in Him. What did they plan? (*v.* 32). So that evening when He came back, He saw the police in the crowd and He knew why. He knew what was coming. So He sadly tells the people: "I shall not be much longer with you on earth. I go my way to——" Whither? What did the hostile Jews think? (*v.* 35).

Did the police arrest Him? Tell me what happened? (*vv.* 45, etc.) Who else stood up for Him? Do you remember Nicodemus before? (St. John iii.) He had not forgotten the young Teacher who so impressed him last year when he timidly "came to Jesus by night." He admired Jesus and had a lingering affection for Him, and at any rate he wanted to see fair play. Tell about him here (*v.* 50) and what the rulers replied. And I am afraid Nicodemus had not the courage to fight for Him further just then. Six months later, when Jesus was dead, we find the good old man coming to bury Him.

§ 5. *Two Startling Pronouncements*

Jesus startled them all greatly next day. You see He was now, as the end approached, beginning to tell who He was. In Galilee He had moved amongst the people as a kindly human friend. They thought Him a prophet for His noble teaching, and they looked with wondering awe at His great miracles. They did not know what to think of Him, only that many of them loved Him. Now it seemed as if He wanted that million of foreign Jews to carry home more solemn impressions—that He wanted the hostile Jews of Jerusalem to know who He was before they killed Him.

The Temple was crowded. All eyes were fixed on the solemn ceremonial as the water and wine from the golden ewer were poured out upon the altar to symbolise the giving of water in the desert long ago, to thank God for showers of water on their thirsty land, and, more than that, to pray Him for showers of blessing on thirsting souls thirsting for God. Then came a dramatic pause as the sacrifices were brought in. And St. John remembers how at this critical moment in the waiting silence rang out a clear, solitary voice. What did it say? "If any man thirst, let him come unto Me and drink. He that believeth on Me out of his heart shall flow rivers of living water." It was the Son of God himself looking on thirsting souls thirsting for God.

And St. John, writing long afterwards, sees the meaning in the light of after events: "This spake He of the Spirit which they that believed on Him should receive."

Why did this startle and anger the Jews? Yes. It seemed an awful thing to say. Was He divine or was He mad? This lone, mysterious prophet saying of God's gift to thirsting souls: If any man thirst, let him come unto Me.

And again at the evening service, He startled them still more. The golden candelabra was blazing with light to commemorate the Pillar of Light which led their fathers in the desert—and in the first waiting pause that clear voice came again: "I am the Light of the World. He that followeth Me shall not walk in darkness, but shall have the light of life!"

Surely these assembled pilgrims had a strange story to carry home. No man had ever heard such words before. And they were not without effect. "As He spake these things many believed on Him. But the others called it blasphemy. They took up stones to stone Him, but Jesus was hidden and went forth out of the Temple."

So ends His first attempt at Jerusalem. He must now flee to the wilderness outside with His little band, and there continue the message that He would leave for the world, which Jerusalem would not hear.

QUESTIONS FOR LESSON I

1. Tell me how and why St. Luke wrote his gospel.

2. Tell of the two books in his baggage.

3. What is meant by the Town Story and Country Story?

4. Who lived in Bethany?

5. Why was the story of the Road six months long instead of a few days?

6. Relate fully the two daring things that the Lord said.

7. What was the result?

THE GOSPEL IN
THE VILLAGES

LESSON II

GOD'S FATHERHOOD

St. Luke XV.

§ 1. Teachings Outside Jerusalem

Now the narrative ceases for the present and for several lessons we follow the teachings outside Jerusalem.

Recapitulate last lesson, briefly reminding why He had to leave Jerusalem. Evidently He means to return at next festival. Meantime for many weeks He is now moving through the country outside, and giving very important teaching. The same thing happened when He was again expelled a couple of months later. We do not always know the exact order of the events or the teachings. So we shall drop the narrative for a while and try to learn the more important things taught outside.

§ 2. The Three Great Parables

We have to depend chiefly on St. Luke and the new stories that he discovered. Now what do you think was

25

the most precious teaching that he found out for his new book? All Christian people would say the three parables in St. Luke xv. I think it was on the road at Jericho that these were said, after the Lord had dined with Zaccheus and the publicans. (See *v.* 1, 2). One feels glad that the Pharisees did grumble, since it got us this delightful teaching about the heart of God. Now name the three parables? Yes. The shepherd who had a hundred sheep, and the woman who had ten pieces of money, and the father who had two sons. And each had lost one, and because it was lost, they were more anxious about that one than about all the rest. You understand that. You would feel the same.

Now what had Jesus chiefly in mind to teach about? The heart of God. It was not the Lost Sheep or the Lost Coin or the Lost Son, but what? The feeling of the person who has lost them. Who is meant by the shepherd and the woman and the man? Our Father in Heaven. God. Be clear about this, and remember that He who told us was the Blessed Lord himself who came from heaven to reveal God's heart to us. So we may feel quite sure about it.

§ 3. The Heart of God

Now suppose a wicked man or woman who had been sinning terribly against God, and now tortured by conscience and very miserable wishes he had not done these things, but feels God must be very angry and must send him to hell—so there is no hope for him. What would these stories of Jesus teach him? That

26

maybe God would not be quite as severe as he feared? That maybe there was a chance that he might some day be forgiven? Is that all he could learn?

Oh, don't you see how much farther our Lord went? He says in the stories: "My son, God has been suffering about you all the time. God is not a big policeman trying to catch you tripping. God is the Father, caring much more than your own father or mother. God, He says, is like that shepherd. What did the shepherd do? Left his ninety-nine sheep who were safe and went away over the mountains in spite of storm and rain and fatigue seeking that lost sheep till he found it. That is God. What did the woman do—a poor woman who would greatly miss that coin? That is what God does who misses that lost sinner. What of the prodigal's father, in his comfortable home with his faithful son beside him and all good things about him? Is he happy? No, says our Lord. He is thinking of his miserable boy in his sin—that is God. The sore heart wanting His child back.

§ 4. Too Good To Be True

Does it seem too good to be true? Why, it is true, even of your own poor father or mother, if you went wrong and broke their hearts. God has put that much of His Nature even into the hearts of poor sinful parents on earth. Do you think your mother would rest satisfied if her other children were good and you were bad and miserable? I remember a mother in a rich, beautiful home who said to me one day: "I never told you my great secret trouble—my boy who went wrong and ran away ten years ago—I don't know to-day if he is dead or alive, but, God help me! he is never out of my thoughts day or night!"

Oh, young people, think of your fathers and mothers! God has given you an awful responsibility, putting your hand on their heartstrings so that with a touch you can give them untold happiness or misery. They can't help it. God made them like that. And from them learn God. Jesus said once to the fathers and mothers in Galilee, "If ye, being evil, cannot help caring like that, how much more the Father in Heaven." If God does not care as much as your mother would, it is a poor business. But if He does? And "much more," our Lord says. Then we are living in a very wonderful world of love with that Father at the head of it! I think hardly anyone would stay away from God if they really believed that.

§ 5. God Seeking

Now there is something more to learn than God's love and pain. What were these people in the parable doing? Merely sorrowing? They were seeking to find what they had lost. "Seeking that which was lost until we find it." Do you think God just waits coldly for His lost son to come back? Or is He seeking? Can you think of any way in which God is seeking to-day? Do you know what usually brings a sinner back? His conscience. The torment of it. Who put this conscience into us?

A man talked to me one day about his evil life. "Are you happy in it?" I asked him. "Happy!" he said.

"No. Sometimes I go ahead without thinking much. Sometimes I lie awake at night and think of my mother and the old home, and think of what I am doing. It is just hell at such times." No, it was not hell. Could you explain it? It was conscience. It was the stern love of God wanting him back, and seeking by this torture of conscience—seeking that which is lost, if so be that He may find it. Conscience is an awful solemn thing, but a delightfully hopeful thing. It means God is suffering for you. God is making you suffer because He cannot bear to lose you. That is what Jesus says. Are you not glad that St. Luke discovered these three lovely parables?

§ 6. God Finding

Now read the ending of each of the parables, about the gladness of God's finding. What did the shepherd say? The woman? The prodigal's father? What does our Lord say about the joy in heaven. Would that make you think at all of pain in heaven. I think it should. For if there be joy with God over one that repenteth, must not there be pain with God over one that repenteth not. But it is the joy we are to think of here. Think of your own father or mother if you went wrong and nearly broke their hearts—if some day you came back sorrowful and changed and started out to live a life that gave them pleasure. Why, that little mother, bowed and troubled, would grow young again in the joy of it. From this learn God.

I was told of a young man who had shamed and made miserable his proud, silent old father. And he used to think of that father cursing him for what he had done. One night, with sorrowful heart, he stole back to the old home, but would not dare to face his father. He thought he would just peep through the window for one look and go away for ever. But he saw the stern old man on his knees, and through the opened window he just heard this: "O God, my heart is sore. Watch over my poor, unhappy boy, wherever he is this night!"

That, says Jesus, is the heart of God.

QUESTIONS FOR LESSON II

1. What was St. Luke's most precious discovery?

2. When do you think our Lord said these?

3. Why should we not think this love and pain of God too good to be true?

4. What do you know of God's seeking?

5. The joy in heaven suggests also pain. Explain.

THE MAN WHO KEPT THE LAW OF BROTHERHOOD AND THE MAN WHO DID NOT

First read of the man who kept the Law of Brotherhood (Luke x. 25-37.)

Now read of the man who did not (Luke xvi. 19 to end).

§ 1. The Father and the Brothers

What was subject of last lesson? The heart of God. The fatherhood of God.

Now can you see that this teaching about God's fatherhood forces us to think about brotherhood between ourselves? Why? Think. If God is our Father, what are we to each other? And if the Father is caring so tenderly for His poor human children, surely it must please Him that they care for each other and surely He must be angry if they bring to each other unhappiness or wrong. So you cannot believe in the fatherhood without believing in God's law of brotherhood. Our Lord was always teaching it. You must forgive your offending brother till seventy times seven. You must be kindly even if he is ungrateful, "for the Father is kind to the ungrateful, and the evil, and sendeth rain on the just and the unjust." "This is my commandment that ye love one another." "One is your Master even Christ, and all ye are brothers."

§ 2. The Man Who Kept This Law

Now we come to the two parables about it. (1) *The man who kept this law.* Tell me the story briefly. That bit of mountain road between Jerusalem and Jericho was about the most dangerous road in Palestine. Just as in London in the stories of one hundred years ago, some of the roads outside were so infested with robber bands that travellers had to go armed and protected—so here. The mountain gorges had robber caves and travelling was very dangerous. Perhaps it was on this part of His road to Jerusalem that Jesus told this parable. You can see the whole picture. The traveller attacked, his attendants running away, the robbers assaulting him, robbing him, stripping him, leaving him half dead.

There he lies in the hot sun by the roadside, bleeding and moaning and hardly conscious. Now comes a Jerusalem priest riding by. He sees the man. He knows he ought to help him. I suppose he would say: "I am in a great hurry. There is no inn here. I could not delay to tend him. And probably the robbers are watching to fall on me, too. At any rate, other travellers will pass who can help him." So "he passed by on the other side." And the Father in heaven was looking. Then comes a Levite, who says the same thing, and perhaps feels that if the priest, his superior, could pass by, he might be excused for doing so, too. Then came a third traveller—a Jew? No, a Samaritan, a race hated and despised by Jews. Surely he might pass by. This wounded Jew would perhaps despise and insult him. But this is a large-hearted, brotherly man. He never stops to think. His kind heart is touched. He is off his ass in a moment, bringing the wine and oil, binding up the wounds, placing him on his own ass, taking him to the next inn, taking care of him, and then, when he has to leave, giving money to the innkeeper to take care of him till he recovers.

Now you remember why Jesus told the story. A man had asked him about religion, and Jesus told him in one sentence the whole of religion. Repeat it (*v.* 27). Yes, to love God with all your heart and your neighbour as yourself. That is the whole of religion—the fatherhood and the brotherhood. But this man has no idea of the great broad thought of Jesus that every man is your brother if you can do anything to help him. "Who is my neighbour?" he asks. Is it relatives or Jews, or people who believe as I do? So Jesus says I will tell you a story. And after the story He asks him a question. What? And the man saw at once. "He that shewed mercy on him." And Jesus promptly replied: "Go and do likewise." That is the law of brotherhood, and only the despised Samaritan had kept it and pleased God.

§ 3. The Man Who Did Not Keep This Law

Now we come to the man who did not keep the Law of Brotherhood.

Perhaps St. Luke knew the previous parable already. He was putting it in his book. Imagine him one day talking of it to some of the old disciples who had been with Jesus on the Road thirty years ago. Somebody asks: "Do you know the other parable that He told us about the unbrotherly rich man and the beggar? It made a great impression on us." (Tell me the story, briefly, of Dives and Lazarus). So St. Luke listens with delight to this dramatic story. He could see it before him as if acted on a stage. There was the lordly mansion and the halls crowded with merry guests and obsequious servants standing around. And the stately host, the "rich man clothed in purple and fine linen faring sumptuously every day." And "the beggar named Lazarus lying at the gate full of sores waiting for the crumbs from the rich man's table while the dogs came and licked his sores." That was our Lord's striking picture of rich and poor in Jerusalem in His day. It is very different in our day? Show this.

Why does the Lord blame this rich man? Was he dishonest? Or cruel? Or otherwise wicked? No, he was just a respectable rich man who probably went to church and paid his tithes and was rather looked up to. Now then, what did Jesus see wrong in him? Just that he had no thought of the Divine brotherhood. He never thought of Lazarus as a brother in God's big family. He did not forbid throwing him the broken meats with the dogs. But he never thought of him as a brother to be considered, to be spoken to pleasantly, or kindly treated. That was his sin.

§ 4. Dives in the Other World

Then the Lord suddenly lifts the curtain again, and shows this rich man in another world. "He died and was buried." That is all his friends saw as they put him in the grave. Is that all Jesus saw? No, he knew all about the other world where the soul had gone to. And he pictures the rich man there. Explain that "hell" here is misleading. It is not hell. It is Hades (see Revised Version), the place of the departed after death. The man is not in hell. But the man is in torment of conscience. That is the meaning of "tormented in this flame." Jesus is always teaching that death is not the end. Life goes on. Character and responsibility and memory and conscience go on just the same. But in the white light of that other world, men see more clearly. There is the poor, little, shrivelled soul in a great, vast loneliness and in torment, for conscience is now awake. The poor, frightened soul is

> Alone, alone with his conscience
> In that weird and lonely place.

§ 5. Loneliness

I should think he would feel awfully lonesome. He would understand the loneliness of poor Lazarus in an unbrotherly world. In the story he sees Lazarus afar off in "Abraham's Bosom." That was the Jewish name for the abode of the good after death. So Lazarus had died, too. In his lonely agony of soul, he cries, "Send Lazarus to help me." But he cannot order Lazarus about now. And I suppose it would not be good for him to be relieved of his misery—at least not yet. He must learn his awful lesson. What does Abraham say? "My son, remember." What does that teach? That we remember in that other world, just the same as here. "Remember your old life and Lazarus. We cannot help you now. There is a great gulf between us."

§ 6. The Great Gulf

Of course there was. There was a great gulf on earth between him and Lazarus and he never tried to bridge it over by kindly words and deeds. There is a great gulf between bad and good people in this world and in that world. And poor Dives learned the awful lesson, *that he who digs a gulf between himself and his brothers is digging a gulf between himself and God.* And nobody crossed the great gulf to relieve the rich man. I suppose that means that in the stern discipline of God that unbrotherly man must stand unhelped in his lonely misery till he learns the lonely misery of unbrotherliness. The story does not say whether that gulf was ever bridged for him.

What does he request about his brothers on earth?

Maybe it suggests that he was beginning to learn about unbrotherliness. For he gets troubled about his

36

five brothers on earth and wants some one sent to teach them. Maybe that means that he was learning. We don't know. We just leave him and all like him sadly and solemnly to the wise mercy of God. At any rate he has been used to teach us a solemn lesson.

"Ye Did It Unto Me"

But we must look at something much stronger still that the Lord said about brotherhood. See his great picture of the Judgment Day (Matthew xxv.) What does He specially emphasise as a reason for condemning or approving? (*v.* 35). He makes you feel that He has been moving beside the lonely people who longed for brotherhood—that He feels their case as if it were His own. The brotherly people did not know that He was looking. And the unbrotherly did not know, either. How do you know? (*vv.* 37 and 44). But He was looking, and He is now. What does He say of it? "I count it as done to myself." He says: "I was hungry and ye gave me meat, thirsty and ye gave me drink, sick and in prison, and ye visited me. Come ye blessed of my Father. For inasmuch as ye did it to one of the least of these my brothers ye did it to me." So you see He is observing to-day how we all keep the law of brotherhood.

"The Sacred Duty of Giving Pleasure"

Now learn this for yourselves—God wants brotherliness. When you grow up, help in all public efforts for the poor and the old and the children. Try always to help others. Try to make people good. And if that is too hard, try to make all about you happy. Be friendly and loving and lovable. For God lays this duty on all poor human brotherhood—*the sacred duty of giving pleasure*. And the Father who is so caring for all His poor children on earth will be pleased if He sees us caring for each other.

QUESTIONS FOR LESSON III

1. How does fatherhood of God teach brotherhood of man?

2. Who was the man who kept the law of brotherhood?

3. Who was the man who broke it?

4. Picture the rich man in this world.

5. Now in the other world.

6. What does Jesus say about brotherhood in his picture of the judgment?

LESSON IV

PEOPLE WHO MAKE EXCUSES

St. Luke XIV. 1, and 7-25.

§ 1. Table Talk

Think of the Lord still wandering in the roads and villages outside Jerusalem. Get this picture in your minds. A dinner party in the house of a wealthy Pharisee, probably in a country town. Friends probably invited with the notice that they were "to meet Jesus of Nazareth." It would be interesting to meet this daring young Prophet who was making such a sensation just then.

During the dinner the conversation got on to the social customs of the time. And Jesus joined in the talk. And men evidently listened with respect. Of course He would talk politely and courteously. But He would talk out straight. Tell me some things that He advises? He advises that guests should not seek the highest places at banquets—that one should not try to outshine others—should think of other people's dignity and comfort and pleasure more than of their own. Then the talk drifted

39

to the silly habit, in Jerusalem and elsewhere, of giving costly, wasteful entertainments to rich friends who are pretty tired of such things and always invite in return to similar rich parties just to boast and show off their wealth and fine houses. And the Lord quite agreed with them. Pleasant little gathering of friends are a happiness, but not these selfish, vulgar parties. Jesus advises: Do things to make people happy. Give pleasant parties to make friends with poor or lonely people who would find pleasure in them.

§ 2. *The Jewish Nation Disappointing God*

But this is not our main subject to-day. I think the conversation was perhaps getting a little awkward and personal. So one of the company tries to turn the conversation with a sudden remark. What? (*v.* 15). Probably just to make talk. Do you think our Lord liked it? Here was He turned out of Jerusalem—in danger of His life because He wanted to bring every one into His Kingdom of God. He must have felt that people who talk piously like that have often very little desire for it at all.

It is like this, He says, "A certain man made a great feast and invited many." You see that is what He thinks of God's kingdom on earth—like a joyous feast to which He invites men and where they would be very happy. What did His parable mean? Who were those invited? The Jews—all through Old Testament days. Then special servants again sent when supper was ready.

40

Who? Perhaps the prophets and John the Baptist, and now the Lord Himself.

Did they come? What then? "Began to make excuse." Jesus warns them that with all their fine talk they were so blinded and so satisfied with themselves that they would make light of God's call to them and excuse themselves and excuse themselves till at last the indignant God should say: "Let them be excused! Excuse them out of my presence and call others to bring in my Kingdom of God!"

Was that prophecy fulfilled? Look at that Jewish race to-day, shut out from their high destiny of bringing in God's kingdom, and we Gentiles called in to take their place. What is a Gentile? Is it Jew or Gentile that is to-day helping the Kingdom of Christ? And it ought to have been the Jews, but for their own fault. That is what gives us our chance to-day.

§ 3. God's Invitations to Us

Now think of this country. Is the Lord's warning needed for any of us? Look at His description of the people invited. (1) They have been invited, (2) and repeatedly invited. (3) They are not a bit afraid of being shut out. How are the people in our country like that? I think that sometimes respectable people who have been hearing God's invitation all their lives are in more danger than heathen or drunkards or people who might be frightened about their chances of getting into the kingdom.

§ 4. *The Excuses*

Now look at the pictures sketched by our Lord of those who "began to make excuse." It might be the one picture of the same person at different ages.

(1) He is young—beginning life—just got married and looking forward to a lovely, happy time. That is just the time when young people should greatly be drawn to the good Father above, who loved them and would make life beautiful for them and make them wise to bring up their children to the beautiful life, too. It is an awful pity at such a time if they turn away from God. "What did the man say?" "I have married," etc. And so God was disappointed.

(2) Now ten years later. In full tide of business. Beginning to make money. What excuse now? Bought five yoke of oxen, etc. He is a farmer—same is true of merchant or a clerk or a foreman in works. He wants to get on. And his wife wants him to get on. Very good thing. Would it spoil their progress if they lived as God's servants? But he politely bows God out of his office or shop. "I know religion is all very good, but I am very busy just now. I pray thee, have me excused." And so the Father in heaven is disappointed again.

(3) Twenty years more have passed. He and his wife are growing older and richer. He has bought a piece of land and must needs go and see it and think what a fine house he can build on it with a lovely view of the river. So he has not time yet. God must be disappointed again.

§ 5. *The Foolishness of It*

What awful fools people are! For what are they asking God to excuse them from? Lord, excuse me from happiness—from a high, noble life—from the deep, glad hope of the hereafter to help me in facing trouble and bereavement.

Ah! it is a poor business. You young people do not know the dreary times that come to older people without religion. And there are worse times, too, when he who has married a wife and therefore could not come stands with that wife—both grey-headed now—at the grave of a godless son or daughter. "O God, forgive us! There was not much in our home to make our children good. We have made a poor thing of life."

And there is a more solemn time still—the first five minutes after death, when that fine piece of land is left behind and the fine yoke of oxen are ploughing for another and the poor soul stands naked and ashamed before God—seeing life's mistake.

Blessed Lord, do not let us be excused out of Thy presence. Have patience with us. Don't give us up. Give us grace, O Lord, not to disappoint Thee!

QUESTIONS FOR LESSON IV

1. What called forth this parable?

2. Show how it applied to the Jews.

3. What is a Gentile?

4. Tell of our Lord's three pictures.

5. Show the foolishness of this conduct.

ABOUT CHURCH, PRAYER, AND BIBLE READING

St. Matthew XXV. 1-14.

Parable of the Ten Virgins. We want this parable here to correspond with that in next lesson. We have to go to St. Matthew for it. It belongs to this closing period of our Lord's life. Probably St. Luke leaves it out as it was already published. It looks forward to the Lord coming back some day—we do not know when—and warns us to watch over our religious life meantime.

§ 1. *The Waiting Virgins*

First tell me the story. Yes. Marriages in the East then and now celebrated at night. The bridegroom, accompanied by his friends, "the children of the bride-chamber," "the friends of the bridegroom" (Matthew iv. 15; John iii. 29; Judges xiv. 11), went to bride's house, and led her with great rejoicing to his own home. She was accompanied from her father's house by her youthful friends and companions (Psalms xlv. 15), whilst others of these, the "virgins" of the parable, met the procession

45

on the way, and entered with the rest into the hall of feasting.

It is very like what happens to-day. Here is an account by a recent traveller, of a marriage which he saw in India: "The bridegroom came from a distance, and the bride lived at Serampore, to which place the bridegroom was to come by water. After waiting two or three hours, at length, near midnight, it was announced, as if in the very words of Scripture: 'Behold the bridegroom cometh; go ye out to meet him.' All the persons employed now lighted their lamps and ran with them in their hands to fill up their stations in the procession. Some of them had lost their lights, and were unprepared; but it was then too late to seek them, and the cavalcade moved forward to the house of the bride, at which place the company entered a large and splendidly illuminated area before the house, covered with an awning, where a great multitude of friends, dressed in their best apparel, were seated upon mats. The bridegroom was carried in the arms of a friend, and placed upon a superb seat in the midst of the company, where he sat a short time, and then went into the house, the door of which was immediately shut and guarded by sepoys. I and others expostulated with the doorkeepers, but in vain. Never was I so struck with our Lord's parable as at this moment: 'And the door was shut.'"

§ 2. *Who Are the Wise and Foolish Virgins?*

Now for the meaning of the parable. Who is the

Bridegroom? Who are meant by wise and foolish virgins? Good and bad people, you say? Do you all think that is quite correct? Why not? Notice first that they all regard themselves as friends of the Bridegroom. Bad, wicked people would not do that. I don't believe He is thinking of the openly irreligious people at all. It is a picture of professedly Christian people, who go regularly to church, and probably say their prayers, and sometimes read their Bibles, and who are not openly showing any disloyalty to Christ. They all seem, to themselves and to others, to be Christ's friends and followers. They all hope to go in with Him to the marriage supper of the Lamb.

Who, then, are the wise and foolish virgins? Better see first what is the difference between them. One set carried a supply of oil for the lamp; the other did not. Therefore we have to ask further, what is meant by (1) the light, (2) the oil. For the first we see our Lord's use of the word "light" elsewhere, *e.g.,* "Let your light so shine before men," etc. The light evidently means the visible side of Christian character, manifested in acts of righteousness. Therefore the oil should mean the inward supply which feeds that light, or, in other words, the grace of God's Holy Spirit.

Now you can tell me who are the foolish virgins. Who? Not Christless, profane, ungodly people. They are people whose light was once burning, who had some inward grace of the Holy Spirit in their hearts; but it got used up, and they did not renew it; those not watchful of their spiritual life, negligent in prayer, slothful in effort, whose religious life is daily dwindling away till it vanishes altogether.

Who are the wise virgins? Those who know that religion means more than religious emotions and feelings, who are earnest, through daily prayer and Bible-reading and sacrament, to nourish with the Divine oil the light of their good life.

§ 3. Both the Oil and the Light Needed

Oliver Cromwell on his death-bed asked his chaplain, "If a man be once in the grace of God, can he ever fall away from it?" "No," said the chaplain. "Then," said the dying man, "it must be right with me, for I know I was once in the grace of God." What should this parable have taught to Cromwell? That for men to be once in the grace of God is not everything. We are brought into God's grace at our Baptism. Many who fall away are brought back into it at conversion. But that is not enough. They are but in the condition of the ten virgins starting out. They are but in the beginning of the life-road. Their lamps are only just lighted. They have to keep in the life-road, to keep up the supply of the oil in their lamps. Whose fault if they do not? God's? No. God's grace is at their disposal all through life. But it must be sought. How? Yes. And men may neglect prayer and Holy Communion and reading of the Bible, and all the means of grace. If so, will the light keep burning till the Master comes? This is a terrible warning, that the light of a righteous life cannot be kept on without taking care of the supply of oil.

But, on the other hand, the oil without being used for light will not do either. The oil is of no use except to produce light. No man can store up God's grace for himself. He must use it. The Bible-reading and prayer and sacraments will cease to bring help if the grace is not being used to do righteous deeds. The supply of oil will fail utterly if it is not being used in the good deeds of a righteous life. We want both the light and the supply of oil to be ready to meet the bridegroom.

§ 4. *While They Slumbered*

Was it wrong? I don't think so. For it is said of both wise and foolish alike—with no word of blame. In the early Church they expected Christ's return every day. "He may come this morning, this evening, any moment." But, as "the Bridegroom tarried," as years and centuries rolled on, the eagerness naturally calmed down, the expectation grew less intense, till now, after nineteen hundred years, we have grown quiet, and calm, and unexcited. We know, as the early Christians did, that He may come any day; but we cannot help taking it more quietly. It is only natural.

And the merciful lesson of the parable seems to be that God wants not so much that we should be feverishly watching, but that we should be quietly ready. True, the more we love Him, the more we shall look forward; but the important thing is that we should so live that, whenever He comes, He should find us ready. Does that mean always in church, at prayer, etc.? No. But doing all our ordinary work as in His presence. Story of Massachusetts senator in time of excitement about Second Advent. The hall grew suddenly dark at midday. Men sprang up in terror. "It is the Lord's coming!" "Well," said the old senator, "what if it is! How better can our Lord find us engaged than doing our duty? Bring in the lights, and proceed with the business."

§ 5. Lessons for Us

Now what does all this teach us? To be careful about our prayers, our church services, our Bible-reading, our Holy Communion, to keep the supply of oil in our lamps.

(1) *Prayer.* Be very careful to say your daily prayers. Never begin a day without coming to God. Sometimes a boy or girl says: "I have to go out to work very early, I have not time." You could make time by getting up five minutes earlier. But if ever you are too much rushed any morning, at least kneel for a moment and say: "O Lord, take care of me and help me to live as thy child this day, for Jesus' sake. Amen." But you ought to say prayers better. (At close of this lesson are a few specimens which teachers might write for pupils to use. There are published little cards of prayers which clergymen can get for them). To say some prayer morning and evening is a most important matter.

(2) *Church-going.* Make a solemn resolution to be always at church at least once every Sunday, and try to learn from the preaching and join earnestly in prayers. And especially be very careful to go regularly to Holy Communion when you are older. That is the closest

of all approaches to Christ. At your confirmation (or if you belong to a religious body where that solemn rite is not observed, but where there is some form of instruction and preparation for Holy Communion) you will be taught about that Holy Sacrament. Here there is only time to remind you (a) that in that sacrament the life of our Lord Himself passes into our lives "for the strengthening and refreshing of our souls," and (b) that He has left it to us as His dying request. "Do this in remembrance of me." (If there is time, read the institution of Holy Communion from one of the Gospels).

(3) *Bible-Reading.* Try to form regular habit of reading some little portion of Scripture every day at prayer time. There are little Bible Union calendars published that would keep your reading regular. Or a good plan is to put your Bible beside your bed with a marker in it and just go steadily on, reading a chapter or even a few verses, moving on your marker, not hurrying or worrying over amount read. Do the Gospels and Psalms first. So by prayer and Bible-reading and the services of the church, keep in touch with God.

§ 6. Suggestions for Prayer

MORNING

1. In the name of the Father and of the Son and of Holy Ghost. Amen.

2. The Lord's Prayer.

3. I humbly thank Thee, O heavenly Father, for

keeping me safe through the past night. I pray Thee to keep me in body and soul under Thy care, and help me to live to-day as Thy child should do. For Jesus Christ's sake. Amen.

4. Make me, O God, really sorry that I so often sin against Thee and of Thy great mercy forgive me. Keep me to-day from all evil thoughts, all bad words, all wrong actions. Make me pure and truthful, honest and kind, diligent at my work and loving towards God and man. For Jesus Christ's sake.

5. Prayer for relatives and friends.

6. God the Father, God the Son, God the Holy Ghost, bless, preserve and keep me now and evermore. Amen.

EVENING

1. In the Name of the Father and of the Son and of the Holy Ghost. Amen.

2. The Lord's Prayer.

3. Examine yourself and give up your account of the day to God.

4. Confess anything wrong and ask His pardon.

5. Prayer for relatives and friends and church and clergy.

6. Into Thy hands, O Lord, do I commend my spirit. Watch over me and defend me from all evil both in body and soul. For Jesus Christ's sake. Amen.

These prayers are to help one who does not know

how to pray. But pupils should be encouraged also to speak to God naturally in their own words.

QUESTIONS FOR LESSON V

1. Who are meant by the wise and foolish virgins?

2. What is meant by the light?

3. What is meant by the oil?

4. How can we keep the oil in our lamps?

5. Tell me about the Massachusetts senator.

LESSON VI

TALENTS LENT US BY GOD

St. Matthew XXV. 14 to end.

This parable was probably taught more than once with variations to fit the hearers. St. Luke gives us one rendering of it here on the Jerusalem Road as the Lord left Jericho (St. Luke xix. 11). St. Matthew has another version which he places a week later. We choose this for its fuller teaching.

Remind of parable of Ten Virgins in last lesson. To-day companion parable. Difference between them, that while the former emphasises keeping the *heart* with all diligence, this has to do with putting that diligence into *work*. That tells of duty of right state of heart while you wait. This tells of duty of *working* while you wait. During the great waiting time between the going away of our Lord and His return, He has given "to every man his work."

§ 1. Setting the Work

First, tell me the story carefully only up to the time that the master "went on his journey." Notice margin of

Revised Version: "bond-servants" = "slaves." Not quite our idea of slaves' work. But would be understood then. I read once a Russian story telling of like conditions. Slaves, if artisans, found work, and paid the master so many roubles a year; if dealers or pedlars, took money, and made profit with it for him. Who are meant by "the master" and the "servants"? What sums did this man give? For what purpose? *For trading*, that they might make profit to enrich their master.

What is meant by talents?[1] Gifts, endowments, advantages, opportunities, given by God to His servants. Have boys and girls got any? Tell me what they are. For this whole story has reference to you. What is meant by the dissimilar amounts? Yes, that God does not start all men equally with brains, or position, or wealth, or opportunity, or even with equal help of His grace. One boy is cleverer, or richer, or in better position, or with more religious influences around him than another. Five talents, or two, or one. Notice that Christ recognises no case of having *no* talent. Every one of you here has something given him by God. (Convince of this before you go on).

All the gifts given for what? For *trading*, to enrich the master. Meaning? That our talents and gifts, and opportunities are not merely for ourselves. God gives them as a means of making profit for Him. What profit

[1] To be perfectly accurate, the natural abilities are not exactly what is meant here. These are rather the "several ability," according to which were given the talents of position, and opportunities, measure of grace, etc. But with young people this is too fine a distinction. It would only puzzle them. All gifts and endowments may be included.

does He want? Gains for himself? Surely not. But God has a tremendous work to do for this poor world to make it happier, and holier, and nobler in every way; and He will not do it except through His servants. If they will not work, all must fail. He has appointed no other way. Therefore are our gifts given. No boy, or girl, or man, or Church, or nation ever received any gift or endowment for himself alone; but that he might with it help others, and make life better and nobler.

Now be clear about this. God has set "to every man his work." What do you think of the person who, at close of life, thinks all must be right with him, "because," he says, "I have never done much harm to anybody." Is that enough? Why not? Why, of course, because God has sent him into the world, not merely to keep from doing harm, but to do work. Fancy a builder coming to his men, and finding them all idle, and boasting that they had done no harm, had not thrown any bricks down on the people passing! How silly it would seem! What is the work set you? At present to be kindly and unselfish, to be earnest in religion, to do your school work and other work given you, and so develop your talents for bigger work hereafter; by-and-by to do your part for God, to help to make life better and happier for men.

§ 2. How Talents Increase and Decrease

Now go on with story. Tell me of the master's return, and the trading servants handing in their accounts. What is meant by the talents increasing to two talents and five talents more? Would they have increased if left unused? Did any of the servants try this? How were they increased? By using. So with all God's gifts. *He that useth increaseth. He that useth not shall lose.* Repeat this three times over for me, all of you. Did you ever see this happen? Blacksmith's great muscle in arm. Why greater than yours? Musician's skill on piano. Savage's keen eye in the forest. The blind man's keen sense of touch, that can distinguish one man from another by touching the clothes. Why all these powers greater than those of others? Because of using constantly. And so with spiritual life. Why is it easier for an old man to love and obey God after doing so earnestly for sixty years of his life? The great Law of Gain in all life—*He that useth increaseth.*

There is also corresponding Law of Loss. Illustrate. We saw gain in blacksmith's arm. Now, suppose instead of using his arm, he had when a boy, tied it up to his side for life? It would shrivel up, muscle would waste away. Compare eye of savage in forest with eye of the mole under ground. The mole is blind. Why? Because never used eyes for generations and generations. God's great law is, "If you don't use, you shall lose." Mammoth caves of Kentucky—great caves, pitch-dark, full of water. Travellers tell us most interesting stories of them. The fish and frogs are quite blind. They have eyes, but quite dead and sightless. Why? Never use them. So if boy's mind never exercised with thought or with lessons, it would become stupid, and finally idiotic. Same of soul's life. If a man never obeys conscience, never thinks of God, never prays, his conscience will get dulled; he will find it more and more difficult to think of God or to pray. Why? State the Law of Loss for me. *He that useth not shall lose.* This is the explanation of many a dead, careless life to-day. It is a terrible warning.

§ 3. *The Master Who Loves To Praise People*

Note in *v. 19, a long time.* Perhaps a hint that the Second Coming was not so near as they thought. What is meant by the master coming back to take account of his servants? When? At his second coming. Tell me accurately the *first* words of the *three* servants? (*vv.* 20, 22, 24). That is, the two first began with glad, grateful acknowledgment that it was God who had given them all they had to begin with. They think of God as the kind giver. The other thinks only of God as the strict, stern demander. That makes a great difference in one's work.

Had the two good servants gained same sum? Yet they got same praise. Why? If each had gained two talents, would praise have been equal? Why not? Does God expect same work from all? What then? Each to be faithful *according to his ability.* Not *quantity* of the work so important as the *quality* and *motive.* So God is very fair and loving to the stupid, and to the poor struggler who finds it hard to do right. "Only be faithful," He says. What is His praise? "Well done, *successful* servant? Or *brilliant* servant?" No, but—*faithful.* We can all be that.

And see in this parable how God loves to praise us. Of course, the work of these men was imperfect.

Fault-finders could easily pick holes in it. But not so God. Hear that hearty "well done!" The generous, hearty praise of Him who loves to praise and hates to find fault. Ah! young people, it is nice to have a Master such as that.

§ 4. *The Reward for Service Is Higher Service*

A very interesting question. When a man has developed his talents and abilities, and spiritual life given to him, what is God's reward? Is it that in the new world after death the men and women should be idlers, and "go out on pension," as it were? Is it that the boys and girls should cease the active life of work, and sit down in a big church in heaven for all eternity? Honestly, should you like that? Well, what is the reward for work? (*vv.* 21, 23). The reward is more, and grander, and higher work. Just as here, when a man has done well in a small position, he gets a bigger position, where he can do greater and more useful work. All who have done useful work for God below, will be rewarded by doing nobler and higher, unselfish work for all eternity above. We cannot tell what endless possibilities of service God has for us.

Young people, full of health and eagerness, could not rest without doing things; and God has eternal doing for them. Heaven is our eternal service, but heaven is not an eternal church service. Nay, there is no church at all in heaven (Revelations xxi. 22), for all life there is so full of God, and of joyous, unselfish work for others in His presence, that we shall not need to come at special times to church to remind ourselves about Him. So live the true, high life here, and it will be true of you what was said of another faithful servant of God at death:—

> "We doubt not that for one so true
> There must be other nobler work to do."

That is the "joy of the Lord," into which we shall enter. The joy of unselfish service in joyous, eternal youth for ever.

§ 5. *The Man Who Would Not Use His Talent*

Terrible warning. Why was this man cast out? Not for doing something terribly wicked, but for leaving undone all that he had been sent into the world to do. What excuse had he? Was afraid. The others had pleasant thoughts of God as a *giving* God. He had only hard thoughts of Him as a *demanding* God, hard to satisfy, who would make no allowances. Some people really have this feeling about God. But most of those who thus fail only use this as an excuse for their slothfulness. They act as if they had no work, and no talents from God. They see wrong-doing amongst their comrades and never object to it. They see efforts after right, and never try to help them. It is a terrible warning that it is not merely open opposition to God that destroys men, but also drifting through life and neglecting to use God's gifts for God's works.

But it is pleasanter to close the lesson with the happier thought of the faithful servants who used God's talents. Thank God that after death life goes on and a new career opens before us of lovely ambitions, of constant, delightful progress. We are going to have "the time of our lives in that wonderful world beyond." "Well done, good and faithful servant, thou hast been faithful in a few things, I will make thee ruler over many things. Enter thou into the joy of thy Lord."

QUESTIONS FOR LESSON VI

1. Tell me the parable of the Talents.

2. What did it mean?

3. Do we all start equal?

4. Is this unfair? See close of parable.

5. What is the Law of the Talents for (1) him that useth, (2) him that useth not? Illustrate this.

6. What is the reward for faithful use of our talents?

7. Will God have work for us in the life after death?

LESSON VII

CHRIST IN THE JUDGMENT

St. Matthew XXV. 31-46.

§ 1. *The Son of Man in His Glory*

After reading the passage go back to beginning. Read twice over *vv.* 31, 32. Try to impress the sublime grandeur of that picture. The Son of Man in His glory and all the angels with Him. Then shall He sit upon the throne of His glory and before Him shall be gathered all the nations of the world for judgment. Tell pupils: Shut your eyes and each try to make his picture of that grandeur and glory.

Now get the picture of Him who was depicting that glory. A poor, hunted, persecuted Man, with the bloodhounds after Him. For the chief priests had just ordered that if any man knew where He was he should tell it that they might take Him and put Him to death. He ought to be frightened. He ought to be despondent. For He had come to found the great Kingdom of God on earth which would take many centuries to accomplish, and before He had got well started they were going to kill Him. Was there ever a more hopeless prospect in this world? And yet He takes it all quite calmly and tells His hearers, One day I shall come in the throne of my glory and all the world shall be gathered before me for judgment.

What must His enemies have thought? That He was mad. What else could they think? No sane man in His position could say such things.

What other explanation could there be? How do we explain it? That He was God Himself come down in human form to teach and save us. That He looked forward calmly to dying for us and going back to heaven, and from thence by means of His servants here carrying on His project of the Kingdom of God on earth and seeing in the future that great day when He on the throne of His glory should judge the whole world. Think of the stupendous wonder of it! Think what you would feel if you stood with Him that day and knew what you know now.

§ 2. *The Farther Horizon*

Now get back to his teaching. Have you noticed in all these teachings how He wants us to keep that Other World always in view, encircling this world as the sea encircles the land? In the parable of Dives, of the Virgins, of the Talents, everywhere everyone is going on to the World Beyond. He always sees the two worlds as one. We only see one and He wants us to keep both in our minds. So in each picture He keeps, as it were, lifting the curtain to give us glimpses of that farther horizon, to keep that Other World always in our minds.

§ 3. Conscience and Common Sense

Here He is telling of the final judgment, telling us that to see our life truly we must see eternity behind it and the kindly, loving, just God looking down on us, and that we must regulate our conduct by keeping in mind the final verdict of God.

Suppose Jesus had never told us about the judgment and somebody asked you, What do you think as to whether there will or will not be a final judgment of men? What would you say? Do you think there ought to be? Why? Think it out carefully. If you were told it would be all the same in the end for Herod and John the Baptist—for some one whom you know who is trying to make everyone happy and some scoundrel who is making people wicked and miserable? What would you say? You would say: Well, at any rate, it *ought not* to be so. Your own common sense, your own conscience would force you to say it. That conscience has been placed in you by God. And Jesus tells you He feels just as you do. One day He says, I will separate them one from the other and put the sheep on the right hand and the goats on the left. They that have done good shall go to the Resurrection of Life, and they that have done evil to the Resurrection of Condemnation.

§ 4. *Judged by What We Are*

In another reference to the judgment (Revelations xx. 12) we read that the Books shall be opened—the Books of our lives, and we shall be judged out of them. When I was a small boy I used to wonder if God kept a lot of big books in which was entered every good or bad thing that I and every other boy did and if He would just count them and send me to the right hand or left. I don't think that now. For I am sure that God has forgiven so many of the bad things when I asked Him for Jesus' sake. I think we shall be judged by what we ARE rather than by what we have done. *By what we are.*

That is a very solemn thing. For we are every day growing towards what we shall be at the judgment. Every day we are growing towards becoming sheep or goats. Every day acts are growing into habits, and habits are growing into character. Every day we are growing into ways of thinking and feeling about certain things—of liking or disliking certain things—of keeping or not keeping God and right foremost in our lives. We are growing towards the right hand or the left. Therefore we ought to give our lives into the loving care of the dear Lord who has so warned us. If we come to Him as His children, He will take care of us and of our judgment. For He will help us to be what He wants us to be.

§ 5. *Jesus Himself as Judge*

Now who shall be the judge? "I myself," said Jesus. The Son of Man in His Glory. I love to think that. For that judgment otherwise would seem an awful and fearsome thing. Even if I should not be condemned, would it not be terrible to think of anyone condemned. It will be awful enough, anyway. But the comforting thing is this. Here is no calm police magistrate coldly investigating, but the divine human Elder Brother, who loves us all and died for us all. Look how on earth He always tried to think the best and hope the best for men. He looked for the smallest good in the midst of their evil. He could see the good motive behind the mistaken action. He could see the sorrow and remorse deep in men's hearts, where others saw only their failure and their sin. Surely it will be awful pain to Him to condemn. Surely in that judgment no one will be lost whom it is possible for Him to save. No one will be lost till the Father has, as it were, put His arms around him and looked him in the eyes with His unutterable love and been rejected.

We must not dare make light of the awful fate of the finally impenitent. But we must always keep in mind that the Divine Brother Himself is to be the judge; that nothing can happen that is inconsistent with the tender Fatherhood of God.

§ 6. "Ye Have Done It unto Me"

What are the chief grounds of condemning or accepting? Here you see again the emphasis that our Lord puts on love and brotherhood. Every poor troubled one, He says, every one hungry or thirsty or sick or friendless or lonely are the objects of His special care. He will count everything done for them or against them as done for or against Himself. It is just what we said in earlier lesson. Love is the chief thing that God desires in us. The sacred duty of giving pleasure is chief amongst our duties. Unbrotherliness is the worst sin.

But the chief thought I want to leave with you as we close this lesson is that the dear Lord Himself will be the judge and that He will do the best possible for every man.

QUESTIONS FOR LESSON VII

1. Show the contrast between "the Son of Man in His glory," and that Son of Man on earth telling about it.

2. What must His enemies have thought of this statement?

3. How do we Christians explain it?

4. Show that the judgment confirms the verdict of our conscience and common sense.

5. Who is to be the judge?

6. What comfort comes from this fact?

ON THE WAY
TO JERUSALEM

LESSON VIII

A SECOND APPEAL
TO JERUSALEM

St. John X. 22 to end.

§ 1. A Nationalist Celebration

Now we are done for the present with the Teachings on the Road. After wandering for a couple of months through the villages teaching and doing His kindly miracles, the Lord is making His second attempt on Jerusalem. And again at one of the yearly festivals. Why? Because then the crowds of Jews from many places would be assembled there.

What was the last festival that He attended? (Lesson I.) You remember how He startled people by some of His utterances? What? And the result was that they turned Him out of the city and threatened His life. Now he is going to startle them again, with the same result.

What is this festival? The Dedication was a patriotic or nationalist celebration, in a smaller degree, somewhat like the American Fourth of July. It commemorated the Dedication of the Temple after the national deliverance of two hundred years ago by their great hero leader, Judas the Maccabee. The heel of another conqueror, Rome, was now on their necks and there were eager patriots there who had taken part in more than one abortive rebellion. That was the trouble in our Lord's mission. They only thought of the Messiah as another deliverer to restore Israel to freedom and glory and they could not understand One whose aim was to raise Israel to be a holy, noble people in a Kingdom of God. The whole country was talking of Him now and it was inevitable that these people at the dedication feast should be thinking of Him.

So Jesus was in the danger line again, staying probably with his friends, Lazarus and Martha and Mary, outside in Bethany after His months of wandering. I dare say they were frightened at His going in to town that morning.

§ 2. "I and the Father Are One!"

Now the excited patriots catch sight of Him walking probably alone in Solomon's Porch, perhaps to shelter from the rain, for "it was winter." "Is this the Messiah, the Deliverer coming on the Festival of the Deliverance? Will He be another Judas the Maccabee?" With their petty little notions they cannot conceive any higher purpose in a Messiah.

"How long dost thou make us to doubt? If thou be Messiah, tell us plainly."

Ah, yes. He is the Messiah come down from heaven with a great high purpose for Israel and the world. But what use to tell these who seek only a leader of revolution? What should it profit a godless little country to win political power for a few years and probably misuse it, as the Romans did. What profit to Israel if it should gain the whole world and lose its own soul?

"Art thou Messiah? Tell us plainly."

"I have told you already," He patiently replies, "and you will not believe Me. If you were my sheep, if your ideals were those of the Father in heaven, you would understand why I am come. My sheep hear my voice and I know them and they follow me, and no one shall pluck them out of my hand. My Father, who has given them to me, is greater than all, and no man can pluck them out of His hand. *I and my Father are one.*"

You can imagine how startled they were, how fiercely angry they were. It was bad enough that He would not lead them to fight the Romans—that He should take this high tone of being sent from heaven to lead them to higher things. But to claim that He was God! *I and the Father are one!*

"Stone the blasphemer! Stone him! Stone him!" The crowd are rushing for the big stones. In that outburst of Eastern rage Jesus stands alone, defenceless, facing death. It seems as if they need not wait for Calvary. The end seems now. But His time was not yet. Something of awe and wonder held back that mob. They must have felt something high and mysterious about that lone Prophet that made them afraid. Later "they sought again to take Him, but He went forth out of their hand." Next time He comes He will let them have their will of Him.

§ 3. Teaching through the Villages

So He started off again on His road, a hunted, persecuted man—surely very sorrowful for His country and His city. Of course He would say good-bye to Lazarus and Martha and Mary as He passed. They would be glad to see Him safe, and sorry that He was going away again. They would miss Him. They did not know then how much more sorely they would miss Him a little later, when a great sorrow had fallen on their happy home. Do you know what sorrow? They knew nothing of that yet.

Now think of Him for another three months on His wanderings, teaching beautiful things about God, doing beautiful deeds to make people happy. And surely being happy Himself in spite of all troubles. One day he healed a poor, crippled woman in a country synagogue, and because it was Sabbath the old country rabbi rebuked Him. And another day He told a lawyer in one sentence the whole of religion. "Thou shall love the Lord thy God with all thy heart, and thy neighbour as thyself." That is the whole of religion, Jesus says. The inquirer asked Him, "Who is my neighbour?" and thus came the Parable of the Good Samaritan. I suppose it would take a big book to tell all that He said and did in those weeks. But we do not know them. Even of those that we do know in St. Luke's notebook we have not time to tell.

§ 4. *The Young Ruler*

One of them we must make time for—the story of "the rich young man who went away sorrowful."

He seems such a fine young fellow, a religious young Pharisee like Saul of Tarsus, trying to keep the outward observances of the law and yet with a yearning desire for a happier, nearer approach to God. We cannot help liking him. Jesus could not help liking him. He could look into his soul and see its desires, its honesty, its strength, and its weakness. The young man came running to Him in his eagerness, and reverently kneeling, "Good Master, what shall I do to obtain eternal life?"

Jesus, beholding him, loved him, and answered: "If you would enter into life, keep God's commandments." But he feels that this is what he had been wearily trying to do for years and not satisfying his soul. You see that to make a bargain with God, to obey commandments in order to get to heaven, is a cold, poor thing, compared with the joyous, happy life of loving and thanking God and like a child just wishing to please the Father.

You see the difference? Of course Jesus wanted him to keep God's commandments. But not as a poor, frightened slave, afraid of God and bargaining anxiously to win heaven for himself by trying to keep a long list of commandments and ordinances of the Scribes and wondering if He could do enough to escape being lost. Jesus' gospel (good news) was a big, beautiful, generous gospel. "My son, God is your Father and loves you now with all your defects and is more desirous of heaven for you than you are yourself. Just trust yourself to Him, and follow Him like a happy, grateful child, and then in happy, grateful love it will be a pleasure to keep His Commandments.

I suppose Jesus saw that the man was in an unhealthy state of mind, worrying lest God should cast him out and that the healthy thing was to stop worrying and by one big act of trust yield himself to God and learn how happy he would be. Jesus knew he had been trying and loved him for it. How should He bring him into the happiness of His kingdom? Nothing for it but to take a great risk with him. "Now have you the courage to do some great thing for God. Go and sell all you have and give to the poor and come and follow Me."

This was a big test. Lay aside your wealth and your honoured position and take your place with the poor, shabby, moneyless followers of a homeless Man. Could you dare that much for the sake of God? I wonder if Jesus thought of him as just the sort of man to make an apostle. If he had accepted, perhaps his name would be familiar to us by the side of Peter and Paul.

For the moment it seems as if he would. He had heroic possibilities. But—but—he cannot decide. He hesitates, with Jesus' eyes upon him—thinks—and hesitates—and fails. "He went away sorrowful, for he had great possessions."

I don't think Jesus would give that advice to every man. Some rich men have done splendid things with their riches. But this was a special case, and He dealt with it as such. Don't you wish the young man had yielded? Perhaps he did afterwards. We know no more about him. But one can't help feeling that one who so attracted Jesus was too high a man to go on as a mere rich man—unsatisfied. I have great hopes that he came back. We don't know. But I don't think he forgot Jesus. And I am sure Jesus did not forget him.

QUESTIONS FOR LESSON VIII

1. Why did Jesus choose festivals for his visits to Jerusalem?

2. How had He startled them on previous festivals?

3. How did he startle them now?

4. What was the result?

5. Tell the story of the rich young man.

LESSON IX

THE RAISING OF LAZARUS

St. John XI.

§ 1. The Message from Bethany

So the Lord parted sadly from the rich young man and went on His way through the roads and frontier villages week after week teaching things which His disciples would remember and tell the world later. One day He was suddenly interrupted by a messenger running post-haste from the two sisters in Bethany. "Lord, he whom Thou lovest is sick!"

The disciples did not mind it much. But Jesus did. He knew that Lazarus was already dead by this time and he thought of the two heartbroken sisters in that home where He had been so happy with them. Perhaps He saw, too, that this was His summons to Calvary. For it was calling Him back to Jerusalem again and He knew that He was soon going to Jerusalem to die.

§ 2. Jesus in Bethany

He went on with His mission—but He was thinking of Lazarus, and two days later He startled the disciples:

"Come, let us go back to Judea again."

"To Judea again! Why, Lord, they have just been seeking to kill thee there. Goest thou thither again?"

How reluctantly they went and how greatly they feared for their dear Master's life we learn from the loyal, desponding Thomas. "He will certainly be killed if He goes to Jerusalem. Let us also go that we may die with Him."

So they went and came to Bethany. In the beautiful springtime, amid the flowers of his garden, Lazarus lay in his grave, and the two sisters were breaking their hearts. Mary was in her room weeping and wondering over the message of Jesus which their messenger had brought back. What message? (*v.* 4) And yet Jesus had not come to save him. And Lazarus was dead. What could He mean, she wondered. Martha, the wise housekeeper, was attending to her guests. Whom? (*v.* 19). The friends from the city who had come to sympathise and condole.

Now someone rushes in. "He is coming! The Master is coming through the village!" And in a moment Martha is rushing down the path. "O Master, if you had been here my brother had not died!"

What did He reply? Did that comfort her much? I don't think so. You see the resurrection of the dead

79

seemed so far away. She thought of Lazarus as dead or sleeping till the resurrection. Was he? No. He was living and thinking and remembering in a great new world. There is no death. The eyes that have closed in the darkness of death open on "a light that never was on sea or land." It is a very wonderful thing to die. I remember a story of a wise old man, an officer in the English army after the Indian mutiny. He was telling of the strange things that happened there—the battles and sieges and hairbreadth escapes. As his friends looked at him and wondered, he solemnly said: "Oh! I expect to see much more wonderful things than those." As he was seventy years old, and retired from service, they stared, and asked him "What do you mean?" "I mean," he said, "in the first five minutes after death."

§ 3. At the Graveside

That was the wonderful life into which Lazarus had gone. The Lord was not thinking of him as a dead man. Lazarus was living then. "I am the resurrection and the life," said Jesus. "He that liveth and believeth on me shall never die." Lazarus was living and was coming back to show it. Poor Martha does not understand but she trusts the Lord without knowing. "Yea, Lord, I believe thou art the Christ, the Saviour of the world." Do you think she guessed what was to happen? I don't think so.

Now Mary is hurrying down. What is her first cry? (v. 32). Evidently the two sisters were thinking the same things. So Jesus comforted her, too. Then He asked a question. What? And they answered? Yes. So they moved together to the garden where the flowers were and the birds, and where also was the dark tomb of Lazarus and the Jewish friends mourning. It was a cave tomb with a great round stone closing it.

§ 4. *"Lazarus, Come Forth!"*

Now you see the crowd around the grave and Jesus with tears in his eyes (how do you know?) and the two sisters frightened and wondering. Do you think the Lord liked bringing back people to life? I think if He did He would have raised many and made many mourners happy. Why should He not? Think for yourselves. Would it be bringing them back to a happier life? You see, Jesus knew about that life beyond and the poor mourners did not. Do you think the people in that world would like to come back? Very few, I think, except for the sake of comforting their friends. But for some reason He decided to bring Lazarus.

Now tell me of His words and actions at the grave. What a fright He gave them at rolling away the stone! Then His thanksgiving. And then the great Lord of life and death uttered His tremendous command. What? And that word of power reached away into the great spirit land and the soul of Lazarus heard it and obeyed. Think of the awful pause at the graveside, the fright and horror and wonder and expectation—eyes starting from their heads as they gazed into the cave. And then—what? And Jesus said? Cannot you imagine the thoughts of the people as they left the garden!

How could Jesus do this wonderful thing? Because He was God come down from that great Other World to us. What delightful lesson did it teach? That there is no death. That our dead are all alive in a wonderful life and could come back to us at any moment if God saw it best for us. Why do you think He does not bring back all our dead as we so often wish? And how did He a little later confirm His great lesson forever? By Himself rising from the dead, just quietly coming back for forty more days to teach His glorious lesson to the world.

§ 5. *The Silence of Lazarus*

Did you ever wonder why Lazarus did not tell everybody about that life where he had been for four days? I wonder, too. Very likely, after the terrible strain of dying, there may be a brief period of repose in which nothing is known and from which one awakes refreshed as a child in the morning. If that were so with Lazarus we could understand. Or perhaps he was so dazed with the wonder of it that he could not find words to tell it. And, you see, it is probably all so different from our life that we probably could not understand. Suppose you tried to tell a blind man about the colours of the flowers and the beauty of the sunset, could he understand? Suppose you tried to tell a stone-deaf man—born deaf—about lovely music. Could he understand? Or if their eyes and ears were opened for a moment and then closed, could they in their wonder tell others what they had seen and heard? Maybe it was like that with Lazarus. We don't know. We can only guess. But we do know of a wonderful world of life and thought and memory and love beyond the grave—and so we are happier about our departed ones—and we are thankful to the blessed Lord who has told us and who brought life and immortality to life through His gospel.

QUESTIONS FOR LESSON IX

1. How did Jesus get the message about Lazarus?

2. What did Thomas say about going back to Jerusalem?

3. Tell of Martha and Mary meeting the Lord.

4. Do you think Jesus liked bringing people back to earth? Why?

5. Can you guess why Lazarus did not tell about that Other World?

LESSON X

COMING BACK TO JERUSALEM TO DIE

St. John XI. 47-57; Mark X. 32 to end.

Too long for class to read. Teacher should read second scripture himself.

§ 1. *Though One Rose from the Dead*

What was last subject? Remember what we thought when messenger from the two sisters reached Jesus in the country village to tell him, "Lazarus is sick"? We thought that this simple message, which the disciples took no notice of, might perhaps really be calling the Lord to Jerusalem to die. Now see how it led to this.

Picture that little crowd at the grave of Lazarus standing stupefied, astonished, as the dead man came back. Then Jesus moving away and the startled sisters taking home the risen Lazarus and the people, too astonished to talk, separating to their homes. You would think they could never go against Jesus any more. But St. John tells us that some were evidently hostile still

84

and went away to report to the Pharisees and priests what Jesus had done. Some people are so bigoted and obstinate that nothing will persuade them. Look what the Lord said one day (Mark xvi. 31): "Neither will they be persuaded though one rose from the dead."

§ 2. *Rulers Afraid*

Next day all Jerusalem is ringing with the news. The people are wildly excited. For Bethany is only a few miles away. This stupendous thing has happened at their very doors. No one could doubt it. Of course it stirred great enthusiasm for Jesus. But it also stirred deep fears in the priests and the rulers.

Why? What were they afraid of? (Get pupils to think and attempt to answer). What did the Jews expect about the Messiah? That He would start a great rebellion against the Roman power and deliver Israel by war and make her a free nation. Many hoped that this miracle would give Jesus a great following and that the whole nation would rise behind Him and fight. But this greatly frightened the priests and rulers. They had seen such rebellions before and knew that the powerful Romans had crushed them with slaughter. They hated Jesus, who had often sternly rebuked them. Now they feared Him as dangerous. They must do something at once.

Of course, Jesus had no such thoughts as they imagined. He had come from heaven to show what God was like, and to found a Kingdom of God all over the world—a kingdom of faithful souls where God should be supreme.

§ 3. "This Man Must Die"

That night a council met in the house of Caiaphas, the high priest. A full meeting. Nobody absent. It was a serious matter, for the great Passover feast was nigh when a million Jews from all over the world would be in the city. No telling what might happen if Jesus, so famous now, should have that multitude following Him.

Read John xi. 47, 48. "What are we doing? This man is doing many miracles. The people are getting out of hand. If we let Him alone all men will believe on Him, and the Romans will come and take away our place and nation." So they argued and disputed. Some said one thing, some another. But the high priest soon stopped that. He had no scruple about going straight to the point. "Ye know nothing about it. There is only one way out. Do ye not see that it is better that one man should die for the people that the whole nation perish not? This man must die!"

See how St. John catches hold of the phrase: "That one man must die for the people." Ay, he says, that high priest told a bigger truth than he meant. How? (John xi. 50, 51).

§ 4. Excitement in Jerusalem

At any rate, from that hour Jesus was doomed. But Jesus was warned and retired away into the wilderness to some place called Ephraim, no one knows where, to spend the few remaining weeks of His life in quiet retreat with His disciples preparing for the end. They needed to hide close this time, for the bloodhounds were after Him; the order had gone out "that if any one knew where He was he should show it that they might take Him."

And in Jerusalem, the excitement grows every day as the Passover draws nigh. It promises to be an exciting, dangerous Passover, especially so if Jesus comes, for everyone has been stirred by the raising of Lazarus. The priests and rulers would like to have caught Him last month to put Him to death. Now that the Passover crowds are coming, they would rather He kept away. It is the one question in Jerusalem for friend and enemy alike. "What think ye, will He come to the feast?"

§ 5. Scene on the Mountain Road

Was He coming? Even while they asked the question the answer was ready if they could see it. Here is the vivid picture, one of the memories of St. Peter which he afterward told St. Mark: "We were in the way going up to Jerusalem and Jesus went before us, and we were amazed and as we followed we were afraid. And he began to tell us what things should happen to Him" (Mark x. 32).

Shut your eyes and call up that picture. The lone mountain road in the wild country of Ephraim; the group of frightened disciples in wonder and perplexity, with their eyes on Him who walks before them, silent and apart. Not like the free, happy comradeship of the old Galilee days. Their relation was changing. For months past their love and admiration have been deepening into solemn reverence. There is a growing sense of wonder and mystery—a sense of His divinity—a sense of some crisis coming. They do not know what to expect. But somehow they seem to have no idea of failure—no idea of death to Him who had just raised Lazarus.

Then He stops to tell them. What? "They shall mock Me and spit on Me and scourge Me and kill Me, and the third day I shall rise again." Of course "they were afraid." But they could not understand. It was unbelievable. He must mean something else. Surely He who had just raised Lazarus could not die now, in the very beginning of His career, when all hearts were throbbing with expectancy of some wonderful future.

Yet it was all true. This was to be the most wonderful Passover of all history—to which all the Passovers for 1,000 years had been pointing. You remember what the Passover commemorated? What? That the Destroying Angel had been passing over the houses of Israel in Egypt and the people had sprinkled the blood of a slain lamb on the lintels and door posts, and so were saved. That pointed as a prophecy to some great deliverance in the future. Now it was to come. The Lamb of God who taketh away the sins of the world was going up to this Passover to shed His blood—to lay down his life for the world's salvation. But this was too great a thing for the poor, frightened disciples to understand yet.

So Jesus walked before them with the great thoughts in His heart on that lonely mountain road going on to Jerusalem. And the great spirit world above and the angels who sang their Christmas anthem on His birthday were watching wonderingly what men were doing to their Lord. And God in heaven kept silence.

§ 6. *All Israel Meeting Him*

Who were coming to meet Him? The whole Jewish race all over the world! Explain? Yes. All the Jews scattered through the earth were crowding in myriads to the Passover. "Parthians and Medes and Elamites and dwellers in Mesopotamia, in Judea and Cappadocia, in Pontus and Asia, in Phrygia and Pamphylia, in Egypt, in the parts of Libya about Cyrene, strangers from Rome, Jews and Proselytes, Cretes and Arabians" (Acts. ii. 9, 10). All unconsciously coming up to meet that lonely Christ coming along the lonely Ephraim road.

Of course they could not understand any more than the disciples, even if they had been told. But think of the impressiveness of it. A million Jews, representing all their race on earth, coming up, all unknowing, to meet that lonely Christ. And as that crowd celebrated the great things God had done in the past, suddenly a great black cross arose in their midst—and they saw, all unknowing, the greatest thing ever done for them, God dying for men!

QUESTIONS FOR LESSON X

1. Why were priests and rulers afraid of Jesus coming up to Jerusalem?

2. Describe their council.

3. How does St. John catch up the saying of the high priest?

4. Tell me St. Mark's picture of Jesus and the disciples on the mountain road.

5. What did He tell that frightened them?

6. Who were unconsciously coming to meet Him?

7. Picture what they saw—the greatest thing God had done for men?

THE END OF THE ROAD

St. Luke XVIII. 31 to XIX. 10.

After reading whole passage, Teacher read *v.* 31-34. Note this is the story pictured so graphically in St. Mark in last lesson (Mark X. 32). Call up that picture.

That is where we left the Lord in last lesson, beginning the sorrowful journey to Jerusalem to die. Now watch them moving along that lonely mountain path. Next day that path opens into the main road from the North—from Galilee to Jerusalem. Many groups of Galileans are passing and the disciples would watch out for northern friends and go on with them, talking of many things, especially of Jesus. Most people are now talking of Him. Now come three pictures of the end of that road to Jerusalem.

§ 1. First Picture

Evening. Groups of tired travellers camping for the night. Capernaum friends get together and Jesus with them. Now in the moonlight see a woman draw near to Him. Who? Where have we seen her last? We saw her

91

walking to church in a street in Capernaum two years ago with Zebedee her husband and her two fisher sons, James and John, to hear the first sermon of Jesus in the synagogue on the hill. (Book I., Lesson IX.) Things have moved since then. The Master is now very famous and thousands are thinking of Him as the Messiah who should found a free kingdom of Israel and deliver the nation from their enemies. So she approaches with a great ambition in her proud old heart. Ambition for whom? I suppose her sons knew what she was coming for.

"Master, will you grant me a mother's prayer?"

"What wilt thou, mistress, that I should do for thee?"

What did she ask for? You see how little she realised what was coming. With kindly pity Jesus thinks what a disappointment is before her and her two boys.

"Ye do not know what ye ask. Are ye able to drink of the cup that I have to drink of, and be baptised with the baptist that I am to be baptised with?"

He looks on the two brave sons, and gravely they reply: "Yes, Lord, we are able."

How little they knew. They thought probably that they might have to fight for Him in the battle with Rome and they were not afraid to fight or to die for Him. And Jesus knew that. A year later, when the disciples were persecuted for His sake, "Herod slew James the brother of John with the sword," and long afterward John died a martyr, loyal to his Lord.

"Ah," said Jesus, "ye shall indeed drink of my cup and be baptised with my baptism of suffering. But to sit on my right hand and my left is not mine to give but it shall be for those for whom it is prepared."

So the ambitious mother went back to her rest sorely puzzled, wondering, questioning. Within a week she knew the answer. You know it, too.

Naturally the others were angry with James and John. But Jesus was very gentle with them. "If ye are to be my disciples do not seek worldly greatness for yourselves. Service is the true measure of greatness. Whoever would be great let him serve most. Whoever would be first of all let him aim to be servant of all. For the Son of Man came not to be served but to serve and to give His life a ransom for many."

What is the world's measure of a great man? Riches, power, success, fine houses and servants, etc.

What is God's measure? Service. To have served others and made life happier and better. That is God's great man.

§ 2. Second Picture

Next day. White sunny road ten miles from Jerusalem. A bend of the road shows Jericho in front, the beautiful "City of Palm-trees," and the Jericho people crowding through the gates to meet the Passover pilgrims. Why? They are expecting Jesus of Nazareth who raised Lazarus from the dead and who is coming, men say, the Messiah of God, to deliver Israel from the

Roman power. They think of Him as Zebedee's wife did.

A blind beggar is nearly trampled by the crowd.

"What does it all mean?" he asks.

"Get out of the way, man!" the people reply. "Jesus of Nazareth is passing by!"

He is not thinking of political or religious issues. He has heard of Jesus healing a blind man in Jerusalem. Instantly a wild hope rises in his heart and his whole soul goes out in a desperate cry: "Jesus, thou Son of David, have mercy on me! Thou Son of David, thou Son of David, have mercy on me!"

The shouts of the multitude are drowning his voice. But Jesus hears it as He always hears you or me or anyone who sorely wants Him. He stopped the whole procession on the spot. "Bring him here to Me!"

And the blind man is led to Him and falls at His feet. Jesus' hand is on his shoulder.

"What wilt thou, my son, that I should do unto thee?"

"O Master, that I may receive my sight!"

"Receive thy sight, my son, thy faith hath saved thee."

"And immediately he received his sight and followed Him, glorifying God, and all the people when they saw it gave praise unto God." And surely Jesus was glad as well as the blind man. Remember Jesus was God. You are looking into the heart of God. That is what God is like.

§ 3. *Third Picture*

The road goes through the main street of the town under the trees. And the town boys are up in the trees watching the excitement. Everyone is crowding to see Jesus. There is a well-dressed man, a government official, trying to see. Why can't he? Little of stature. Why will not the people make room for him? Because they hate him. He is a publican—the collector of taxes in Jericho. You know how the Jews hated these publicans who were often dishonest and oppressors of the people.

You remember the tax collector in Capernaum whom Jesus called to be His disciple? I think this fellow officer of his in Jericho knew all about this and wanted to see Matthew's friend who was not ashamed to talk with publicans. I think that, like Matthew, he wanted to be good, and was ashamed of his trade, a lonely man with no good friend to talk to. If he could only speak to Jesus! If he could even see Him? What does he do? Climb up into the trees with the boys. It looks rather ridiculous, but he does not care. Down deep in his heart is a longing for Jesus.

Then came the surprise of his life. What? Jesus looked up and spoke to him, as if He had come specially to meet him. "Zaccheus, come down. I want to stay at your house to-day." I wonder he did not fall off the branch with surprise. There he learned what the blind man had learned, what you and I and all of us can learn, that no poor soul can ever long for Jesus without Jesus knowing.

And Jesus stayed with him and ate and talked with him. Don't you think Jesus knew the evil in him? Yes. But He knew the good in him, too. Think what it meant to his poor lonely heart to have a friend who could understand and trust him, who could understand not only the evil but the craving for good. Surely Zaccheus would never forget that night he had spent with Jesus. Perhaps he never saw Him again on earth. A fortnight later he heard how his new Friend had been put to shameful death in Jerusalem. Have you any doubt that Zaccheus became His faithful disciple? What did he say as He bade him good-bye? "Lord, from this day forward the half of my goods I will give to the poor, and if I have wronged any man I will restore him fourfold."

That is what "coming to Jesus" means, not mere beliefs or pious words, but a whole life changed into honourable, noble deeds.

That is all we know of Zaccheus. Here is an old legend about him that I have somewhere read. A very aged man, little of stature, every morning tending the ground around an old sycamore tree near Jericho. "Old man," said a passing stranger one day, "why carest thou thus for that old sycamore tree?" "Because," said the old man, and his eyes grew young as he said it, "from the boughs of that tree I first beheld my Lord."

You remember the three loveliest parables in the gospels. The Lost Sheep, the Lost Coin, the Prodigal Son? (St. Luke xv.) I think we got them through Zaccheus. For

St. Luke places them in this period of our story. And I know the Jericho people were angry at Jesus eating with a publican, and you see (Luke xv. 1) the parables were told because of somebody grumbling that he should eat with publicans and sinners. If we are right in this, the world should be very glad that Jesus met Zaccheus.

Don't forget that that same Lord is looking down on us to-day, and wanting us all to love Him and be happy like Zaccheus.

Now we have reached the End of the Road. Next time we see Jesus He is entering Jerusalem to die.

QUESTIONS FOR LESSON XI

1. Where did Jesus and His disciples meet old friends from Capernaum?

2. Now describe the first picture.

3. Now the second.

4. Now the third.

5. What did blind Bartimæus and Zaccheus learn about Jesus that we all should learn?

6. Tell the Legend of Zaccheus.

7. Why do you think the three great parables in St. Luke xv. were probably told here?

PALM SUNDAY AND THE CHILDREN

St. John XII. 1-8; St. Luke XIX. 28-44.

§ 1. Anointing by Mary of Bethany

Now we have reached "the end of the road," the six months travelling through the roads and villages outside Jerusalem, the frustrated attempts to teach in the city—the dangers of a persecuted Man with His enemies watching Him. Jesus is now going into Jerusalem for the last time—going in to die.

Where did last lesson leave Him on the road? What happened there? Now from Jericho He and His disciples go on with the great pilgrim procession to the Passover, up the dangerous road to Jerusalem where the traveller in the parable (Luke x.) fell among thieves. Now they have reached the village of Bethany. What friends live there? The Bethany people are crowded on the roadside, for they too have heard of the coming of Jesus and everyone wants to see him. Now He sees the friendly faces of His Bethany friends and leaves the procession and goes home with them.

This is on the "Friday, six days before the Passover" (John xii. 1). Friday night at six o'clock the Sabbath begins, His last Sabbath on earth. It ends at six o'clock on Saturday. So that evening, Sabbath being over, there is a supper in His honour, and "Martha served and Lazarus was one of them that sat at meat" (*v.* 2). The disciples are present. Notice amongst them that gloomy, red-haired man who is to win undying shame ere the week is out. Judas Iscariot is a bitter, disappointed man. He is clever enough to see that Jesus is going to disappoint them, that He has higher thoughts than battles and glory and wealth and power, and deliverance from the Romans. So Judas is bitter and disappointed.

Now Mary comes in to the feast all pale and troubled, for she suspects that the Lord must die. She kneels behind him and pours her costly vase of ointment on His tired feet to do Him honour. It is all she can do. Who objects to this, and why? He is in bad temper and looking to find fault. What does Jesus reply? "She has done it for my burial." Ah, if they knew that within a week He would be lying dead, I don't think anyone there would have agreed with Judas.

§ 2. *Palm Sunday Procession*

Next day is Sunday. All Bethany is excited and proud. The most famous person in the land is their guest, and everyone wants to see Him. And the disciples are excited and proud. Surely great things would happen now. Fresh excitement when Peter and John told them: "We are sent in Bethphage for a young ass on which never man sat. The Master is going to ride to-day in procession to Jerusalem."

So the procession starts, every face bright with enthusiasm and expectation. Except one. Whose? The Lord Himself. There is something sad in His look. Not like a king riding in triumph to victory. Rather like a disappointed king riding to His death. He knows.

One sometimes wonders why He thus rode in. It is not like Him. It marks a curious change in His attitude. Up to this we have read of His retiring from notice, of His forbidding people to tell of His cures, of His general desire to avoid unnecessary publicity. Now we have the very opposite. He is actually arranging for a public procession into Jerusalem, just when the whole place is full of excited crowds at the Passover feast. Evidently He has some great purpose in view. Does He want to escape the Cross and be carried off by the enthusiastic crowd to be made king in the palace at Jerusalem? Surely not. For what has He told His disciples? (xviii. 31). He has come up to die. But before He dies, He must make a last appeal to the nation, whose chief representatives are now up at Jerusalem at the feast. The nation must have one more chance of accepting Him before it is too late.

Tell me about His arrangements? (*v.* 30). Without any spies He could see what was at Bethphage; without any army He could make men obey His bidding. He could know everything and do everything. His procession was not a very grand one. Not stately horses and chariots and guards of soldiers. Just a young Galilean teacher riding on an ass, the symbol of peace, and with a shouting crowd behind Him. (Point out that in the East the ass is a finer animal than ours—even kings rode on asses in peaceful processions). Would it mean anything to the Romans in Jerusalem? Why should it be so impressive to the Jews? Because the Jews knew by heart the chief prophecies about the Messiah; and almost every Jew who saw Jesus that day would think of the famous prophecy in Zechariah. Read it for me (Zechariah ix. 9). Remember that there was already wild excitement about Him. The people on all sides had heard of His miracles. A crowd had gone out to Bethany the day before to see Him, and see Lazarus, whom He had raised up (John xii. 9). Now another enthusiastic crowd from the city is coming to meet Him. All men were asking whether He was the Messiah. So this is His public claim. His public assertion, "I am the Messiah; I am the Christ who was to come."

Did the crowd believe Him? Yes. In no other way can we explain that wild enthusiasm that stirred the whole crowd. They flung their clothes on the ground for Him to ride over; they tore down palm branches to strew in the way. They shouted with eager excitement the words that could only mean welcome to the Messiah. For the time, at least, that huge crowd of people believed that Jesus was the promised Messiah. It was a great day for Jerusalem. For the moment it almost seemed as if they would recognise their King, and yield themselves to the beautiful life of unselfish devotion to which He called them. It is a very wretched thing to go near to accepting Christ as our King, and then to stop short. Many do. I think it is a very sad thing to look at a multitude gathered in worship on Sunday, and to see them all the rest of the week rejecting the Lord. And a very sad thing, too, to think of a class like this, learning about Jesus now, interested in the story, and some of them in their later days going away from Him altogether. I don't like to discourage you, but I want to warn you. I have known bright, pleasant boys and girls who once seemed to care for the Lord, but who are now, I fear, utterly gone from Him. Pray to Him that it may not be so with you.

§ 3. Sorrowing over Jerusalem

What were the multitudes shouting in their joy? What sad vision did Jesus see in His mind as they turned the corner of the hill and beautiful Jerusalem came into view? He sees the doom of the nation and His heart is sore that He could not save them and their beautiful city from that doom. Oh, if they had only received Him sent down from heaven to make them a holy nation and their city the centre of the spiritual Kingdom of God in the world! What is His sorrowful cry? "Oh, if thou hadst known," etc. (*vv.* 42-44).

Ah! He knew. Men in that crowd would forty years later see their nation wiped out, their lovely city destroyed, and its people crucified or sold into slavery. I suppose in the noise not many heard His words. So they went on shouting and cheering and the crowd of pilgrims in the city turned out to hear the shouts: "This is Jesus, the prophet of Nazareth of Galilee!"

§ 4. *The Children in the Temple*

I wonder what they expected at the end of the procession. Perhaps that by a mighty miracle He who had raised Lazarus from the dead would drive out Pilate and his Roman soldiers and begin to found a glorious kingdom for Israel. But He had no such thought. He had come up to die and by dying teach the world how much God cared for them and so found a kingdom of servants of God, a kingdom that is going on to-day and shall go on for ever. Each one of us that joins it is spreading it on earth.

So when the crowd stopped near the temple He entered.[2] And I think there was a great Passover children's service going on. For I read (Matthew xxi. 15-17) that the children in the Temple began to shout "Hosanna." I think they had heard the crowd shouting "Hosanna to the Son of David" and they were so excited at seeing Him in their midst in the church that they tried to shout it too. The priests were angry and bade Him silence them. What did He reply?

I think simple young children can get closer to Him than anyone else. They are so innocent and unsuspicious and so attracted by affection. And I think He loved

---

[2]I am omitting here the cleansing of the Temple, as St. John places this in an earlier visit from Galilee, where we have already dealt with it. We are not quite sure where to place it. Some think it happened twice but it does not seem probable.

best being with children. Mention some of His sayings which suggest that.

QUESTIONS FOR LESSON XII

1. What happened the night before Palm Sunday?

2. Tell of Judas that night.

3. Describe Palm Sunday procession.

4. What was the sorrowful picture in Jesus' mind?

5. Tell about children in the Temple.

LESSON XIII

WARNINGS IN THE TEMPLE

St. Matthew XXI. 23-43; XXII. 15-41.

No time to read both these sections. Teacher should summarise the second while pupils follow with open Bibles.

Keep in mind that we have now come to the week of the Passion, the last week of our Lord's life on earth. Last lesson told of the triumphal entry on Sunday. We now go on at the rest of the week. Notice, still the change in His attitude. All must now be public and open, and courting, rather than avoiding, notice. No longer doing good deeds quietly and telling men to keep silent about them. No longer avoiding conflict with the authorities. It is full time now to bring matters to an issue. This week brings the crisis of the fate of the nation. They must be made now, in full, clear consciousness, to accept or reject Him. It must be made impossible to ignore or overlook Him any longer.

Palm Sunday is over. In the evening Jesus returned to Bethany to rest with those dear friends, Martha and Mary and Lazarus. Next morning He is back in the

Temple. Monday and Tuesday He is publicly teaching. Wednesday He seems to have spent quietly in Bethany or in solemn farewell talks with the disciples. On Thursday He came in to keep the Paschal Feast. His farewell supper with disciples. On Friday He was crucified.

§ 1. Conflict with the Priests

There is not time for all the solemn teachings in the Temple. We confine ourselves to the chief day, Tuesday, a terrible day of strain and conflict for Him. When He came to the Temple this Tuesday morning, who met Him? Of course they were very angry. Remember Jerusalem crowded with people for Passover. Temple crowded. He had dared to teach publicly in Temple. What do they ask? "By what authority," etc.? Do you see any trap in this question? Probably expected Him to say He was God, and then could charge Him with blasphemy. Did He? No.

"Before answering," said He, "I should like your opinion about something. What? Why was this difficult? (*vv.* 25-27). But what had this to do with their question about His authority? Don't you see? (1) All held John to be a prophet inspired of God. (2) John had borne witness to Christ. He said: "I am nobody—only a voice in the wilderness. I have only come to prepare the way of the Lord. He that cometh after me is mightier" (Matthew iii. 11-12). "Behold," cried he, pointing to Jesus—"behold the Lamb of God" (John i. 29-36). Therefore, if they said John's mission was from Heaven, He would reply, "Why, then, do ye not believe his statement that I am the Messiah?" So you see why they dared not answer. Therefore He would not answer them. Did they deserve an answer? Why not? If they had been true, earnest men, who were in doubt about Him, would He have treated them thus? Surely not.

§ 2. *The Two Sons*

Tell me this parable. Of course it was aimed at the audience before him. Who was the certain man? What classes meant by the two sons? The first think themselves very religious, talk about God and religion, and go to church, etc.; but *do* nothing of God's work. Second class, the openly irreligious, who did not at all profess to do God's work until something touched them, and they "repented and went." Which class did the priests belong to? How did He make them condemn themselves?

What is the lesson of this parable for us? That our WORK is the important thing, not our thinkings or feelings. If we are not DOING anything to help make life happier and holier for others, it is no excuse to say we like going to church, or that we wish we were better, or that we admire unselfishness, and think it is very lovely. The world is full of sin and trouble and social misery. When you get bigger, you will find Temperance and Missionary and Social Service work, and religious work of every kind waiting to be done, and being largely left to clergy to do. When you see that, it is a call of God to you, "Son, go work in my vineyard." But what can you do in vineyard now? Learn lessons well and so prepare for future usefulness. Help to make school life and home life pure and unselfish. Be brave enough to stand out against comrades if anything mean, or false, or impure is being said or done, etc. All this is work in God's vineyard. He is so wanting to make a noble, beautiful world, and He likes to let us all help.

§ 3. *The Wicked Husbandmen*

What sort of mood do you think the chief priests and elders are in now? Very angry? Yes; but also, I think, a little bit cowed and subdued. All their imperious domineering had failed, and with the crowd listening and, I suppose, enjoying it, they had to stand silent and listen like children to His stern teaching. He had been so gentle always before, that they hardly know Him now. Like a lion roused, something in His look and manner awes them. So, before they can recover from rebuke (*vv.* 31, 32), He turns on them again. "Hear another parable." Tell me this parable accurately. Who was householder? Vineyard? Jewish people. Out of the great wilderness of the sinful world, God had, as it were, walled off one corner, where the plants should be specially tended and cared for. Were Jews more tended and taught than other nations? Yes. No other nation on earth got such care, and teaching, and help of every kind to be religious. Was this because they were special pets and favourites, and that God did not care much for the others? Certainly not. Impress on pupils that it was *for the sake of all the rest* that the Jews were trained, that they might preserve and hand down religion through all the world. This is most important. The idea of God's favouritism for some peoples and neglect for others must never be entertained.

What should have been the result of all this care? Was it so? No, Jews thought they were God's special pets, and instead of trying hard to be deeply religious and so help others to be so, they were content with listening to the prophets and reading the Bible, and going to church, and not *doing* anything. Just like a vineyard absorbing all the water and manure, etc. into the soil and bearing no fruit.

Did God really go away? (*v.* 33). Where else does Christ say the same thing? (Matthew xxv. 14). What does it mean? Not *really* absent—is near to every one who wants to be helped; but His visible presence and miracles, etc., withdrawn, so that men should feel free to act as they thought best. Who were the servants? Prophets, good kings, etc. What did God send them for (*v.* 34). *Fruits.* What does it mean? Yes; just the same as in Parable of Two Sons. Fruits of a good, true, beautiful life, which God sought. How treated? (*v.* 35). (See also Matthew xxiii. 34; Jeremiah xxxv. 15; Acts vii. 52, etc.)

Now comes something very touching (*v.* 37). Why touching? Because He was talking with calm sadness of what He knew would be done to Himself in a few days. Does He put Himself down as one of the servants, merely a prophet like other prophets? No. The Son—the Son of God. Though so gentle and modest always, He never drops this claim. And He seems to say, too, "This is God's final and greatest message." Last of all, He sent His Son, as if He would say: "God has no more now that He can do. He has made His last move. He has no other messenger, no other inducement. If men will not be touched by that, their case is hopeless." Show me again how He makes the priests condemn themselves. Notice the simile of the great Foundation Stone, which now lies in the way of all men to be built upon. And if they will, like negligent builders, leave it about unused, they will fall on it and hurt themselves. All who know about Christ and try to ignore Him will surely hurt their souls. But there is always a chance of remedying this until the end, when it is too late, and the Christ whom they have ignored and neglected shall come in judgment, like a great stone falling on the wicked.

§ 4. Laying Snares for Him

No time to do more than touch remainder of His teaching. Just summarise it for you. Keep Bibles open. In the evening His enemies came back, trying "to ensnare Him in His talk" (Matthew xxii. 15-41). You see, Palm Sunday had frightened them. Jesus of Nazareth was evidently more powerful than they thought. "The whole world is going after Him," they said. So they thought if they could discredit Him with the people or get Him into conflict with the Roman government they might weaken or destroy him.

So they try a clever trick. "Master, is it lawful to pay tribute to Cæsar?" You see the trick? If He said Yes, the people would be angry. If He said No, Pilate and his soldiers would arrest Him. But He answered wisely. What?

Then the Sadducees, who mocked at the resurrection, came laughing at Him about a fancied case of a woman who had been married seven times. Now who shall be her husband if there be a resurrection? Jesus answered, Ye do err, not knowing the Scriptures. In the resurrection they neither marry nor are given in marriage, but are as the angels of God.

Then the Pharisees tried again. Of the 513 precepts and commandments of the Law, which is the greatest? What a noble answer they got! "There are only two real commands of God. First, Thou shalt love the Lord thy God with all thy heart; and second, Thou shalt love thy neighbour as thyself. There you have the whole essence of religion." Surely the whole crowd felt the nobleness of that answer.

Then Jesus walked out of the Temple—never to enter it again.

QUESTIONS FOR LESSON XIII

1. How did the Lord spend each day of Holy Week?

2. Tell me some of the clever tricks to ensnare Him in His talk.

3. Tell Parable of the Two Sons and show its application to the Jews.

4. Also parable of the Wicked Husbandmen.

5. What was His great answer to the question about the chief commandment of the Law?

LESSON XIV

FOUR SCENES
BEFORE THE END

St. Luke XXII. 1-21.

Later in course of lesson, teacher himself (to save time) read for the class St. John xiii. 1-15.

Scene I, Tuesday

Tuesday night. The night of that day when He had so sternly rebuked the Pharisees and priests. Caiaphas' house near the Temple. Conspirators gathering in one by one out of the moonlight. Pharisee, Sadducee, Herodian, Priest and Scribe, Annas and Caiaphas, bigots and atheists, all banded together in conspiracy against the young Teacher, Who had dared everything for the truth. How fiercely they hated Him! Such men as they could never forgive Him.

Not merely that they thought He was endangering the political existence of the nation. There was personal hatred besides. They had been defeated and shamed in open encounter in the presence of the people. They had been shown up as ignorant and hypocritical. This uneducated young Rabbi from the country had turned on them as a master would turn on a crouching slave and lashed them with these terrible, scathing woes, that they, or the people who heard them, could never forget. He had been so gentle up to this time that they never dreamed that He could turn on them like that. Never could they forgive it. Die he must. But when? Not on the feast day. Wait till the people dispersed, and only a few disciples with him. It must be soon, but not on the Passover. Ah! but it must be on the Passover. Why? Probably at that moment He was telling His disciples. "Ye know that after two days is the Feast of the Passover, and the Son of Man must be betrayed," etc. He had quite settled that during the Passover, when they commemorated the slaying of the Paschal Lamb in Egypt, must be slain the great Paschal Lamb, of whom this was but a type and shadow.

And now comes a marvellous over-ruling of evil to bring about God's purpose. Even while they were discussing it, something happened to make them do it at Passover. What? A knock at the door; a message brought in: "A disciple of Jesus the Nazarene is outside." Just what they wanted. "I will betray Him unto you in the absence of the multitude. I know His secret places of prayer—haunts at Gethsemane and elsewhere. What will ye give me?" What did they give? Yes—seems very little—perhaps only an instalment; perhaps with the Jewish bargaining spirit, they beat down his price by saying that they could easily get Him without any guide a few days later. At any rate, the bargain was made, the

114

blood-money paid over, and the Holy and Just One was sold, just when He was out alone at Bethany praying for the poor sinful world that He had come to redeem. Think what an awful state of mind Judas had brought himself to before he could do that! We shall consider this later.

Scene II, Wednesday

Jesus alone in His little room at Bethany, preparing for the end. He seems to have spent all the Wednesday and Thursday in deep seclusion, preparing, we may believe, for the terrible struggle of Gethsemane and Calvary. We may feel sure that, as on that other night, a crisis in His life, "He continued all night in prayer to God."

Don't miss the contrast. Look at the two pictures. In the one picture the chamber of conspirators—scribes, and priests and Pharisees; the chief laymen and the clergy, the leaders of the people, with wealth and comfort, and earthly prosperity, and power to destroy the man whom they hated. In the other picture, a hard-handed young carpenter, poor and despised, and hated, and about to be to-morrow execrated by the mob and murdered by the law; with nothing to comfort Him but the calm sense of right and duty, and the deep consciousness of the Father's presence and approval. Which would you rather be? Though all the comfort and wealth on the one side, and all the discomfort and poverty on the other? Yes. Learn thus in what consists the true value and nobleness of life. For it was not because He was divine that He could endure so nobly. It is the grace given to every true heart who dares everything for the right.

Scene III, *Thursday Night*

Teacher here read himself (to save time) St. John xiii. 1-15, or perhaps better read it after the picture.

Jesus and the disciples assembled at Last Supper. This is the night of the Paschal feast and the disciples had asked that morning, Where wilt thou that we prepare? What did He reply? Why did not He tell them straight out where to go? It suggests the caution of a hunted man in constant danger, afraid of being arrested before the time. Nobody must know. Especially Judas must not know beforehand. Peter and John do not know as they set out. "Go into the city where the women come from the wells. Note the unusual sight of a man bearing a pitcher." This is the secret sign probably arranged with the host, who was evidently a disciple of His. The man is watching for them and will go on without speaking. "Follow him to the house where he entereth in."

When the hour was come, He sat down and the twelve apostles with Him. The farewell supper after these three happy years together. There is an especial tenderness in His heart to-night. "Jesus knowing that the time was come that He should depart to the Father, having loved His own He loved them to the end." "With desire I have desired to eat this Passover with you before I suffer." "Ye are they who have continued with Me in My temptations."

Even then they were disappointing, striving each to get the best place at supper. Jesus said nothing, but watch Him as "He ariseth from supper and took a towel and girded Himself and began to wash the disciples' feet and to wipe them with the towel." In Eastern feasts of rich people there would be a slave to wash hot, tired, dusty feet. There was no one humble enough to do it here—except the Lord of the Universe, who had often taught them that the greatest is he that is most willing to serve. Surely it touched and shamed them. Think of Him washing their feet! Think of Him washing the feet of Judas and the secret horror of the traitor who knew where those feet had taken him last night! Surely if tempted again to strive and to be selfish they would remember that lesson their dear Lord had taught them.

Scene IV, *The Same Scene Still*

A little later. The Lord and the Twelve sitting, or rather, reclining, at the Passover. Explain the way of reclining round the table. It is their last night together, and they are saddened and troubled. And He, too, is burdened in heart. Think of the sorrow to Him who knew all things. Knew that these twelve whom He had chosen to be His closest friends would all fail Him— Peter deny—Judas betray—all the rest run away from the danger and leave Him. How that great love was disappointed then. And now also. But he is thinking of their sorrow, not of His own. St. John tells us how He comforted them (St. John xiv. 1). How like Him—never to think of Himself, but only of others.

Suddenly a startling announcement: "One of you shall betray Me." Did they suspect Judas? Or each other? Wonderful humility and brotherliness. Each only mistrusted himself. "Could it possibly be me? Surely none of us would do it!" Judas, too, asks, "Is it I?" He wants to see if the Lord is as unsuspicious as his brethren. And in a low voice unheard by the others, Jesus answers him. He would not shame him publicly. He would help him still to repent.

Now wine-cup passed round. Bread and bitter herbs eaten. Now a pause. Something very solemn happening. What? Describe whole act for me (*vv.* 17-21). He was now putting an end to Jewish Passover. It had pointed in type to Him through all the centuries. He was the Lamb who should be slain. You remember what Passover commemorated? The destroying angel passing—the lamb slain and the blood sprinkled on doors that they might be safe. It was a type looking forward to the blood-shedding of Christ to save men. And now the type was about to be accomplished and done with. Instead of it, He would make new and different festival. He took plain bread and plain wine and blessed them, and by His mighty power decreed that when this was done by His Church in the days to come, it should be a means of our receiving spiritual strength, receiving in some wonderful way His own self into our souls. You can't understand all this mystery; but you can understand at least two reasons why people should be regular at Holy Communion, and why you should when admitted to it.

The first we have mentioned, "The strengthening and refreshing of our souls." The life of Christ passing into our lives to make us pure and strong. Thus the Holy Communion is a tremendous power. It is God's nearest approach to us on earth. It is "God's kiss" to His dear children on earth. Surely people should not miss that. What is the second reason? This: "Do it always," He said, "in remembrance of Me." "Don't forget Me. Let this be always the reminder to you of My love, and of the lives I want you to live for Me." Imagine a dying mother saying to her children: "Do this or that in remembrance of me. Once every month put fresh flowers on my grave." What a shame if neglected! How it would disappoint and sadden her if she could know. But that is a common sin with careless Christians. Think of this when you see the Holy Table arranged for Communion, and let it remind you of that night in upper room, and of the many who, by their neglect, disappoint and sadden the Lord. Say, "Lord, help me not to sadden or disappoint Thee. Lord, when I am old enough to be allowed to Thy Holy Table, I will try to go regularly in remembrance of Thee."

QUESTIONS FOR LESSON XIV

1. What is subject of each of our four scenes?

2. On what day did each take place?

3. Why was this secret sign of the man with the pitcher?

4. Tell of the Lord and Judas at Last Supper.

5. What was the lesson He taught in washing the disciples' feet?

6. What are the two chief reasons for coming to Holy Communion? (Emphasise this lesson for pupils.)

THE TRIAL AND
THE CRUCIFIXION

GETHSEMANE

Read St. Matthew XXVI. 30 to 46.

Glance at St. John XIV. to XVII.

We are now drawing near the end. We are in presence of an awful mystery—the Great Deliverer needing deliverance—the Comforter of humanity looking for comfort. Be very reverent and solemn. Make the pupils feel that they are on holy ground. Teacher should spend much time beforehand in meditating and praying about this Lesson, and trying to enter into the solemn spirit of it, that his subdued tone and manner may express his inmost feelings. The long speech and prayer in St. John are of course too long to read. But they are very important. Teacher should study them carefully beforehand and decide what parts to comment on while pupils hold Bibles open at this place. It should occupy about half the time of lessons.

Recapitulate last lesson. Last Supper over. His good-bye to them. Had told them of parting—tried to comfort them about the future.

§ 1. The Farewell Prayer

(Glance at St. John xiv. to xvii. and keep Bibles open there.) To fully understand and enter into any scene in the Gospels, it is necessary to put together all the accounts of it. For instance, in this Lesson. We thought last day about the sad farewell meeting in Upper Room and the Institution of the Last Supper. But the story did not leave the impression of a long night sitting, of long, loving, sorrowful conversation hour after hour, closing with an earnest prayer of the Lord for His poor disciples whom He was leaving.

Now read Matthew xxvi. 30, and then the corresponding verse, John xviii. 1—"When Jesus had spoken these words." What words? You look back in St. John's account (*ch.* xiv., xv., xvi., xvii.), and a whole new light flashes on the scene. You see after the institution of the Holy Communion they did not go out at once. For hours they sat on in sad communing together, as the Lord poured out His soul to them, and they saw how deep was His love, how touching His utter forgetfulness of self. All "these words" in St. John come between *vv.* 29 and 30 in St. Matthew's account, but St. Matthew does not record them. So before going on to the Gethsemane story we should spend a little time on these farewell words and prayer of Jesus. Glance at these chapters in St. John. *Teacher, having studied them beforehand, should here comment reverently on these words, picking out the most striking verses while pupils keep Bibles open.* "Let not your hearts be troubled." "I will not leave you comfortless." "I will send the Comforter." "I will come again to receive you to Myself," etc. And they sit listening like men around a friend's death-bed. And then when it is time to go, there is the solemn hush of expectancy. They see by His face that He is about to pray. I think there must have been tears and sobbing as they heard that prayer, so full of its exquisite sympathy and self-forgetfulness. All for them and for the future Church. (Read a few verses of the prayer, John xvii.) He knew of the wretched morrow—the betrayal and denial, the judgment, the mockery, the spitting on, and scourging, the awful agony of the Cross. But no thought for that, only for the lonely little band that He was leaving, and the future that lay before His infant Church. He was always like that. Utterly unselfish, utterly self-sacrificing. He is like that still in heaven to-day.

§ 2. Gethsemane

Now return to St. Matthew. "When they had sung a hymn," probably the *Hallel*, the usual Passover hymn comprising Psalms cxiii.-cxviii. Read a few verses of this hymn. Then out in the bright moonlight they go along the Olivet road. The strain on His heart growing more severe—the intense craving for solitude—for prayer—for the Father's presence. He must be alone in His favourite praying-place. Talk on the road. Peter's impulsive reply. What? What was Jesus' sorrowful prophecy of him? Did Peter think such a thing possible? Peter always impulsive (see again *v.* 33)—big, generous, impulsive heart, always rushing at things, not calm and quiet. Very confident. Not safe to be too confident. Safer a few hours before when he distrusted himself, and said, "Lord, is it I?" Be afraid of unaided self. Be very confident in God.

Now approaching very solemn sight. Right on to lonely glades of Gethsemane. All left behind but three. Who? When with Him before? Why bring them? His human craving for friendship in great trouble.

Verse 37. "He *began* to be," etc., as if a sudden wave of emotion breaking over His soul like a huge breaker sweeping in suddenly from the sea. "Sore troubled," restless agitation, intense mental distress. He who had been so quiet and self-possessed just before is now seized in the pangs of an uncontrollable anguish. How terrible it must have been when He, so reserved usually about Himself, so unwilling to talk of His own pains or discomforts, has wrung from Him the unutterably pathetic cry, "My soul is exceeding sorrowful, even *unto death,*" *i.e.,* "I Who know the limits of human endurance, feel that I am touching the very borders of death—just a little more, and my life would give way." And then notice in His deep trouble how touchingly He reaches out for comfort and sympathy. "Keep near Me, you three. Tarry you here," etc. As they tarry, He hurries past. He must be on His knees. He must flee to the Father's presence for comfort and help. What blessed thing for anyone to have such a love of prayer and of God. Good for us if we on gain for ourselves such a blessed shelter in trouble.

§ 3. The Agony

Now we behold awful sight. Agony of mind so intense that even He could not bear it. He Who was so brave and calm to bear everything. Listen to tortured cry: "Oh my Father! if it be possible, remove this cup from Me." Meaning of "cup" (See Mark x. 38, 39). What was this cup? Was it only the fear of death? Was it only the denial, betrayal, contempt and scorn, awful death upon Cross, with mocking crowds around? Surely not. Bad as all these were, He was too brave to fear them. Even some of His humble martyrs have borne death without fear. What was it? We do not know. Cannot understand. Deep mystery of God. We only know that it came in some way from the awful burden of the sins of the world. Read Isaiah liii. 4-6, "The Lord hath laid on Him the iniquity of us all. All we can see is that it was some awful, intolerable agony of soul that came on the pure, holy Saviour from bearing the horrible burden of the world's sin.

Was it easy for Him to bear it? No. He had laid aside His Divine power—had to bear it as a man. You and I find it hard to do painful things for the sake of God and duty. Wonderful and comforting to think, He found it hard, too. Terribly hard. "If it be possible, let it pass from Me." How awful it must have been! Is it wrong to feel it hard to do one's duty? No. Duty is all the grander when you feel it hard and yet do it. The Lord had to force His human will to obey the Divine will, just as we have to do. But He determined to do it, however hard. That was the grand thing. Therefore He can understand our struggles to do it. Can sympathise with and pity us and rejoice with us when we conquer like Himself. If He had kept His power as God to help Him, would it be half so grand or so helpful to us? What does He say about getting His own will? (*v.* 39). Thus comes the end and relaxing of the struggle—the end of the agony and bloody sweat. The cup cannot pass. Then said Jesus: "Father, if this cup cannot pass from Me except I drink it, Thy will be done." And the storm ceased and there was a great calm in His soul. No matter how hard to do or bear, let that be always our prayer. When it comes to praying that, the struggle grows quieter. Like as with our Lord, there comes a great calm—the calm of victory—and "there appeared an angel from heaven strengthening Him." So with us, too.

§ 4. Sympathy with the Sleeping Disciples

How many times did He go to see if disciples were keeping watch with Him? Why? His heart yearned for their comfort and sympathy. And what did He find each time? Yes. They failed Him—miserably, shamefully. Was He very angry? No. Would you be, if some day in horrible misery you found sisters or mother quietly sleeping while you were suffering! "Much they care," you would say, angrily. You would not trouble to make allowances or excuses for them. Not so Jesus Christ. See what He says (*v.* 41): "Ah!" He says, "the spirit is willing enough; it is only the flesh that is weak." He knew it was not that they did not care, but they were so dead-tired—severe nervous strain all that night—perhaps up previous night with Him as well. Is it not touching to see Him actually apologising for them, making excuses for them, trying to look for the good in them, where others would only see the evil? Is it not comforting to us to think He is like that—like a father with bad son looking for any little trace of good in him, delighted to find it, making every allowance for him—looking for the good motive at bottom of mistaken action—looking for the sorrow and penitence in his heart, when others only see his faults and his sin. Thank God we have such a loving Master. But never forget how much He suffered for us.

> "I bore all this for thee,
> What dost thou bear for Me?"

QUESTIONS FOR LESSON XV

1. Show the place in St. Matthew's story where we should insert the farewell words in St. John.

2. Can you remember some of them?

3. What do you think the Lord so shrank from in Gethsemane?

4. What brought Him peace in the agony of His struggle?

5. What led to His prophecy about Peter's denial?

6. Show His sympathy with the sleeping disciples.

JUDAS AND ST. PETER

St. Matthew XXVI. 57 to XXVII. 7.

§ 1. Arrest

Briefly remind of last lesson. The Lord of Glory struggling in His agony like any poor, human man. "Father, if it be possible, let this cup pass from me!" Then the final victory of His will and the end of the struggle, the relaxing of the tension. "Father, if this cup cannot pass from me, Thy will be done!" And immediately the storm of His soul ceased and there was a great calm, "and there appeared unto Him an angel from Heaven strengthening Him." Ah, these angels were watching over their dear Lord better than His disciples were. Since that Christmas night three and thirty years ago when they sang their angel anthem as the little Baby appeared on earth they were watching with wonder and sorrow what men were doing to their Lord. They knew why He had come to earth and they adored Him for it. But they had to see very sorrowful things.

Where were the disciples all this time? Fast asleep,

though they knew that His enemies were hunting for Him and that they should have watched. Now they have slept too long. The danger is on them. He himself is the first to see it coming, the flashing of lights, the sound of rough voices, the youth in his white night robe racing to warn them (Mark xiv. 51), the Sanhedrim police drawing near through the trees "with lanterns and torches and weapons." Rise! wake up! he that betrayeth Me is at hand!

Judas has chosen his time well. That midnight visit to Gethsemane gave him his chance. The disciples are caught off guard and surrounded. And now the traitor, throwing off all disguise, comes forward into the light. In all the infamous story of Judas is nothing more infamous than his signal to the police. "Whomsoever I shall kiss that same is He. Seize Him and hold Him fast." And he came forward to his Master in friendly greeting. "Hail, Master," and kissed Him! Sternly the Master looked him in the face. "Judas, betrayest thou the Son of Man with a kiss!" Surely, as the disciples said of him later, Satan had entered into him.

But the disciples themselves had not much cause to boast. Jesus said to the soldiers: "Ye seek Jesus of Nazareth. I am He. Ye have no charge against these disciples. Let them go their way." So they let them go. And they went! Though Peter rushed in blustering to slice off Malchus' ear, panic seized them all. It is hard to believe it. It is horrible to believe. "Then all the disciples forsook Him and fled."

§ 2. The Trial in the House of Caiaphas

So the Prisoner is led away, majestic, alone, with the rough grasp of police on His shoulders. Through the darkness of the midnight they lead Him to the house of Caiaphas, the high priest, where the scribes and elders were gathered together not to judge but to condemn Him. For they had already decided His fate. You remember what Caiaphas had decreed already? (John xviii. 14). So you see what little chance there was of a fair trial.

Now see the most astonishing sight in history. The Judge of Mankind at the judgment bar of men! The Saviour of Mankind about to be killed by those whom He came to save! Think, what a mockery. His judges are the men who hated Him for rebuking their sin, the men who sent out spies to trap Him, the men who tried to kill Him. Could these men, with their spite and cant and hypocrisy and self-seeking, form any true judgment as to character of the loving, self-sacrificing Christ? No more than a bat could judge the sunshine. They called witnesses—for what? to find out the truth? (*v.* 59). Determined that He must die. Little they thought that thus they were doing what He wanted. He, too, was determined that He should die.

Now get the class to picture the place that we may see the scene of Peter's denial. As the police bring their prisoner they come (1) to the *porch* with pillars and porter's lodge. (2) Through this they pass into the *courtyard* open to the sky, where happened the scene of Peter's denial. (3) Beyond this, reached by steps, the

JUDAS AND ST. PETER

judgment room. There were the judges. There came Jesus, pale and tired, with strong cords binding His hands, while without in the *courtyard* Peter and the servants were warming themselves at the fire. It seems that when all the disciples fled, Peter and John were ashamed and came back (John xviii. 15) but afar off (Mark xiv. 54). The doorkeeper knew John and let them in.

Now see the trial. Tell me about the false witnesses. Did they succeed? It seems as if He would get off free. They could not condemn Him. Was high priest pleased to see it? (*v.* 62). Could not sit still—so angry at his failure, and calm, dignified silence of prisoner. "Why don't you answer?" he cries. Could He have explained this story about Temple? But He knew it would be no use. They only wanted an excuse to condemn Him. Did He get fiercely angry? Did He ever in His life get fiercely angry? Yes (Mark x. 14); but it was for other's sake, never for His own. He could be fearfully angry at one who had led a little child astray; but He could be grandly patient and silent when they were cruelly ill-treating Himself. What a beautiful soul was His! He is trying to make us like that. Are *we* trying? At last the high priest gets an answer. Stung beyond endurance at the quiet silence of the Lord, he asks—what? I adjure thee by the living God, etc. (*v.* 63). No more silence now. Calmly, solemnly, the answer comes: "I am." And what more? How grand, how God-like, the answer. What a mean, unjust trial! If He had said "No," they would say "an impostor." He said "Yes," and they cried what? Thus was He condemned to death. Then comes the horrible, brutal treatment. We almost shrink from reading it. Fancy those brutal creatures cuffing and boxing Him; spitting in His face; tying bandages across His eyes in mockery to make Him guess who struck Him! Oh, how could they? And He was their God! Their Saviour!

§ 3. *The Testing of Peter*

At last they have pronounced His condemnation and gathered what evidence they could for the final trial before Pilate in the morning, for it is not lawful for the Jews to put any man to death (John xviii. 31). Only the Roman governor can pass the death sentence.

Now they march down the steps, down into the courtyard on the way out. And there in the courtyard is the frightened Peter. Another trial was going on down there. Peter being tested. Poor Peter! He found it much easier to be religious and confident before the danger came: Remember the Lord's warning last night and Peter's confident reply? (*v.* 33). We never know ourselves till tested. Ashamed of running away, he had come in now, and tried to seem at ease, sitting with servants at fire, but very frightened. Would they find out about Malchus' ear? Suddenly, without preparation, his testing begins. How? (*v.* 69). Did you ever tell a lie when suddenly asked, and you had not time to decide? So Peter now. A sudden temptation like that is a good test of us. Cultivate habit of bold, transparent truth always, and then you will never be taken unawares. Then he tried to escape this girl; out into the porch, where the groups of people waited. But the girl followed him and repeated the charge. What happened? (*v.* 71). How did the third suspicion come? Galilean accent—country brogue. Peter, now utterly terrified, cursed and swore that he did not even know Jesus! What a horrible thing! (*v.* 74).

So God's testing of Peter was over. Peter had shamefully failed. Oh, how could he! With the Master who loved him being persecuted to death, and all the world against Him, would it not be better to suffer anything rather than desert Him? And in a minute he saw this himself. In the cold, grey dawn outside he heard the cock crow, and just then they were hurrying out the Lord, condemned to death. And as He passed out He gave Peter that one look of unutterable pain that nearly broke poor Peter's heart. And Peter remembered the word of the Lord, Before the cock crow thou shalt deny me thrice. "And he went out and wept bitterly."

Could Christ ever forgive such a sin? Such sorrow as Peter's will always bring forgiveness. St. Clement tells that Peter never forgot this sin—that whenever he heard a cock crow, he would get out of his bed and cry again to the Lord in shame and tears. See how sweetly the Lord forgave him. Even on the cross and in the Hades world He was thinking of poor Peter. Think of the touching message He left with the angels for the women at the tomb: "Go and tell my disciples *and Peter*—Peter, who has denied Me—Peter, who is breaking his heart, and thinks I have cast him out for ever—tell him especially." Oh, no wonder Peter was so fond of Him. No wonder that burst of eager, passionate devotion: "Lord, Thou knowest all things; Thou knowest that I love Thee!" (John xxi. 17).

§ 4. Judas

Peter was watching what men were doing to his Lord and now was in awful misery over his sin of shameful denial. Did you ever think that there was probably another disciple watching, too, in still more awful misery for a greater sin? Who? (xxvii. 3). "When he saw that he was condemned." I suppose he did not expect it. Thought, perhaps, that they would not dare to condemn, or that He, with His Almighty power, would blast them with a look if they touched Him.

You can imagine him skulking about the courtyard, keeping out of sight of Peter and John; waiting for news of the trial; hearing the priests, perhaps, ask for himself as a false witness against Jesus, and keeping out of their way or refusing to come forward. Perhaps he saw them buffet Him, and spit on Him, and use Him so shamefully. And then at last he hears to his horror that they have actually gone so far as to condemn Him to death! Poor Judas! he had been fearfully wicked and treacherous; but the remorse of that hour must have been a terrible retribution.

What did he do? (*v.* 3). Can't you imagine him rushing up to the priests with wild and haggard face: "Take back your money! take back your money! Oh, I have sinned! I have betrayed the innocent blood!" Can't you imagine the cold sneer of those cruel hypocrites who had no pity on him any more than on his Lord.

What was their reply? I think he must have been half mad at the moment in his terrible remorse. I wonder he did not spring on them and rend them. What did he do? In his rage, dashed down the money, ringing and clattering, upon the marble pavement, and rushed away madly to hang himself. Oh, wretched Judas! Don't you wish he had rushed up to Calvary instead and thrown himself for pardon at the foot of the Cross?

So the Lord went to His death with sorrowful thoughts about His closest friends. The Twelve had forsaken Him. Peter had denied Him. And Judas—I think the Lord's keenest pain was in His thoughts about Judas.

QUESTIONS FOR LESSON XVI

1. Tell story fully of Peter's denial.

2. Describe place to show how Jesus overheard him.

3. How did he show his penitence?

4. Tell of trial in the house of Caiaphas.

5. What drove Judas wild, and what did he do?

LESSON XVII

THE ROMAN TRIAL

St. Matthew XXVII. 1-2 and 11-31.

Teacher should study also the corresponding accounts in St. Luke xxiii. and St. John xviii., xix. and weave into the story.

§ 1. Pilate

Remember subject of last lesson?

You know why there had yet to be a final trial before a Roman judge? The Romans did not allow any subject people to pronounce the death sentence (John xviii. 31). That was reserved for Rome. So in the early morning about seven o'clock that procession of priests and elders, leaving Peter and Judas, moved on the Prætorium where Pontius Pilate, the Governor, held court. This was the trial which should decide the Prisoner's fate.

Soon the Governor takes his place in the Judgment Hall, ready to judge one of the usual Passover riots, as he thought. What sort of character do you think Pilate was? Strong or weak? Brave or cowardly? He was afraid of the Emperor and afraid of the mob. Once he had insisted on setting up the Roman standard in Jerusalem, and the mob yelled round his house for six days, till he gave in and removed the standard. Another time they complained to the Emperor about some golden shields that he had set up; and again, at another time, when he used the money of the Temple Treasury for building a watercourse, the priests and the people made such a disturbance that he was forced to give it back.

So you see his weak indecision made him a poor judge to have to try a prisoner whom the mob wanted to condemn. Yet it is only fair to say that his sympathies were with the Prisoner.

§ 2. *The Trial*

Teacher should read and try to piece together the accounts from the other Gospels. Any "Life of Christ" would help. Trial opens with the question, "What accusation bring ye against this man?" and the reply, "If He were not a malefactor, we would not have delivered Him unto thee." But such vague charges will not do. Must be more definite. Then arises the chorus of complaints: "He perverteth the nation"; "He forbids to pay tribute"; "He says that He Himself is Christ, a King!" This is coming to the point which the Governor can understand. So he questions Him.

Something in the bearing of the Prisoner seems to have impressed Pilate. He evidently did not believe the accusers at all. Why? (*v.* 18). He knew that bitterness and bigotry would attack any man who ventured to think for himself; and it was clear that the Prisoner before him was of the sort who would not only think for Himself, but would die for His thinking if necessary. Perhaps his Roman training made him feel for a brave man in misfortune. Perhaps there was more than this. A superstitious fear seemed to grow on him, that this was something more than an ordinary brave man. At any rate, he wants to acquit Him if he can. What does he ask Him (*v.* 13). But no answer still. Pilate marvelled greatly. He knows the man is innocent, but he can get no answer from Him.

Then he seems to have taken Him aside in private (John xviii. 33), to ask Him, wonderingly, about this Kingship. "My Kingdom is not of this world," was the calm reply. "Art thou a King, then?" "Yes, I am a King; King of all truth-seekers. Every one that is of the Truth, every one that wants to follow the highest Right, is My subject."

This is too high a teaching for Pilate, but it certainly is not the teaching of a political rebel; so he goes out and says to the accusers: "I find no fault in Him." Then arose an uproar that frightened him. "He stirreth up the people from Galilee to Jerusalem!" Pilate eagerly catches at the word "Galilee." It offers him a chance of escape. "Is He from Galilee? King Herod of Galilee is in the city; send Him to him." So he thought to escape responsibility. Perhaps the Galilean king will be interested in this Galilean prophet and express an opinion. But that wily old Jew was too clever to be caught. He was not going to mix himself up in a treason trial. And the Prisoner's lofty attitude vexed him. Jesus would not open His lips to the Baptist's murderer. So Herod and his officers set Him at naught and put an old purple robe on Him in mockery of His Kingship and sent Him back. There is no escape for Pilate that way. He must make his own decision.

§ 3. Pilate's Wife

Pilate is now more troubled than ever. As he took his seat a page boy enters with a message from his wife. What? (*v.* 19). To a superstitious Roman this would be a very evil omen. Pilate would know of the murder of Julius Cæsar and the strange dream of Cæsar's wife, which might have saved him if attended to. He is greatly disturbed. How can he escape condemning that "Just Man"? What is his next attempt? In a weak moment he appeals to the people. There was a custom that at Passover to please the people he should release one prisoner at their request. So he puts the question to them. What? (*v.* 17). And they reply with a shout, Barabbas! Barabbas! Barabbas! Pilate is disappointed. Then in his perplexity he utters aloud the question that had been troubling him all the morning. What? (*v.* 22). "What then shall I do with Jesus, who is called the Christ?"

The mob knew very well what they wanted done with Him. The fierce cry rings out: "Let him be crucified!" Ah! but they had not the troubling thoughts about Him that Pilate had. This silent Prisoner has strangely impressed him. He has talked to Him and conferred with Him. He does not know what to think of Him. He has never seen any one like Him before. There is a look in those eternal eyes that he cannot understand, attracting him towards something beautiful, and high, yet repelling him with a sense of awe and mystery. His wife's strange dream, too, stirs superstitious fears in him. But the shouts go on: "Crucify Him! Crucify Him!" Pilate's temper is roused. "I will not crucify Him. I will scourge Him and let Him go."

§ 4. The Guardroom

So the order goes to the guardroom, and soon the white, exhausted Prisoner is strapped to the scourging post and His blood is flowing and His nerves quivering under the brutal lash. Then a horrible, almost incredible scene. The brutal guards have got the Prisoner to themselves. Good jest to make fun of Him as King. So, after the horrible scourging, Herod's old purple cloak is thrown over His bleeding shoulders, and they place Him on a raised seat, in mockery for a throne. And they bow the knee before Him, saying, "Hail! King of the Jews." Then a new idea strikes one of them, and he climbs down into the garden to tear off a bough of sharp-thorned acanthus, and twist it into a wreath, and, amid loud, brutal laughter, the pale, silent King is crowned and sceptred. They thought all this would vex Him and make Him angry. Did it? Could anything make Him angry? Ah! yes. But not anything done to Himself. If they put a stumbling-block before His little ones (St. Matthew xviii. 6); if they injured the helpless, or neglected the needy, that would make Him terribly angry. But the cruel injury to Himself only made Him deeply sorrowful for the men who had fallen so low.

It always irritates cruel people if you seem not to mind their cruelty. So they got angry and violent. (See *v.* 30). We can't speak of it—it was unspeakably horrible. But suddenly they got a fright. In the midst of their brutality they looked round, and lo! Pilate, the Governor, has come in, and sees it all. At once the brutal horseplay ceases, and Pilate (I think to move the compassion of the mob), brings forth his pale, brave Prisoner so cruelly outraged (See John xix. 1-16). What result? Nothing but a wild outburst of rage from the chief priests and officers. "Crucify Him! Crucify Him!" That was Pilate's last effort, and it failed.

While he hesitated still, a clear, accusing voice rang out across the court. "He ought to die because He made Himself the Son of God!" The Son of God! "Then was Pilate the more afraid and entered again into the palace and asked Him, Whence art thou? But Jesus gave him no answer." It was too late for answers now.

§ 5. *Pilate Washing His Hands*

There was nothing else for Pilate to do now except what a brave man would have done at first. And Pilate could not nerve himself to that. So he took water and washed his hands as a protest before the multitude. "I am innocent of the blood of this just person. See ye to it."

There are cowards still in the world ashamed to stand up for Christ. Be always ashamed of being a coward, like Pilate. He knew Jesus was innocent. He did not want to condemn Him; but he did not dare to face opposition for sake of doing right. And that want of daring to do right has branded him with eternal shame. There is a legend that his ghost still walks on Mont Pilatus, in Switzerland, in the moonlight, always hopelessly washing his hands. No use to wash his hands, or assert innocence of the "blood of this Just Person." Obstinately that blood has clung to him through all the ages since. All over the world to-day, every little child who can say the Creed, repeats, "Suffered under Pontius Pilate."

QUESTIONS FOR LESSON XVII

1. Why was this further trial of Jesus?

2. Describe the character of Pilate.

3. How did he feel towards Jesus?

4. Where does King Herod come into the story?

5. Are there cowards like Pilate to-day? How?

LESSON XVIII

THE CRUCIFIXION

Luke XXIII. 26-47, and Matthew XXVII. 39-44.

The direction for the Gethsemane lesson applies still more here. Do everything to get class into right attitude of solemnity and reverence. It would be intolerable to have a careless, flippant class at this lesson. Teacher might well use the prayer aloud at the beginning: "O Saviour of the World, who by Thy Cross and precious Blood hast redeemed us, Save us and help us, we humbly beseech Thee, good Lord."

§ 1. Calvary

Remember last lesson? The timid Pilate too cowardly to save Him when he saw that he could prevail nothing, "delivered Jesus to be crucified." And straight from the Roman tribunal the Son of God went forth to die.

Then the hot, wretched walk to Calvary. Jesus struggling to carry the cross and fainting under its weight. No wonder, after that awful night and morning. Who carried it with Him?

The details of the Crucifixion are very awful, but the chief impression left on us is the grand, calm patience of the Lord. The brutal soldiers strip Him, and then squabble over the dividing of His clothes, like the relatives of a dead man over the property left behind. He stretches Himself, as directed, on the cross, and the great spikes are driven through His quivering limbs; and then He is lifted up to be exposed to the crowd and mocked at in His terrible agony.

Notice the different classes who stood around that cross? (Matthew xxvii. 39-44). (1) Of course the disciples and friends who were breaking their hearts for Him. (2) The people who "stood beholding," many of them surely in sympathy though they had not the courage to rise in insurrection and tear asunder priest and Pharisee and soldier ere a hair of His blessed head were touched. (3) The passers-by, out for a holiday to see an execution, who were sneering, If Thou be the Son of God, come down from the cross! (4) The cruel priests, who were gloating over their revenge. They had never forgiven Him for His terrible exposure of them in the Temple, for His words of blame and awful warning. Now was the hour of revenge. Even the two robbers, perhaps two of Barabbas' band, joined in their cruel taunt. What was it? (*v.* 42). "He saved others, Himself He cannot save." Was it true? Yes. Far more true than they could understand. How? He must choose between Himself and us. If He is to save us, He cannot save Himself. And where Jesus Christ is concerned there can be but one decision in that choice. What? Ay, never did He think of Himself from the cradle to the cross. His whole life was one long self-sacrifice for others. His death must be the same. "I lay down My life for My sheep."

§ 2. *"Father, Forgive Them"*

Is it not awful to think that men could treat Him thus? That many to this day are mocking and neglecting Him, giving Him more pain and sorrow? And is it not very touching to think of the sweet, tender patience of Christ? It is just here comes in the first of the "voices from the cross," as He looks on the heathen soldiers and the thoughtless, sinful crowd. He makes all allowance for them. They are ignorant, they are excited just now, they don't know what they are doing. He prays not for vengeance on their cruelty, nor for deliverance for Himself. What? (Luke xxiii. 34). Think of the generous nobleness of such a heart as that. If that nobleness does not subdue our hearts, nothing else will.

I wonder if the crowd heard that prayer. I think, at any rate, that God heard it on their behalf. See how they were touched (Luke xxiii. 48). Did the brutal soldiers? One of them reached up a sponge with wine to relieve His thirst, and their centurion and his fellow soldiers were so impressed with all they saw and heard (Mark xv. 39; Matthew xxvii. 54). Even for the wicked, bigoted priests, I think, it was heard (Acts vi. 7). Let us think of Christ's prayer, and be thankful for it, and be touched by that tender love and pity, that exquisite unselfishness, that at such a time could forget Himself to pray for others, even for His enemies.

§ 3. The Dying Robber

One man at least heard it. With astonishment and awe. (Here read Luke xxiii. 39-43). Both joined at first in the mockery, "If Thou be the Christ save Thyself and us. Now one is growing silent. I see him grim, stubborn, scowling at the crowd, too busy with his own pain to think of another's. Then that brave, silent dignity of Jesus begins to touch him. His heart misgives him. He is ashamed of himself and of that brutal crowd mocking a helpless man. And then—the tremendous thing happened. Jesus speaks and the robber holds his breath as he hears—not a cry of pain nor a curse such as came easily to his own lips. "They do not know what they are doing. Father, forgive them." Behold a miracle! In an instant the man is changed, suddenly converted! The beauty of the Christ character has done for him in a moment what all the remedial legislation of the Empire had failed to do in years—wakened him up to shame and sorrow for his past and a dim dawning of reverence and admiration. And with it awe and wonder about this Messiah crucified for calling Himself the Son of God. Who is He? What is He?

He turns indignant on his mocking companion. "Dost thou not fear God? We deserve to suffer, but this Man hath done nothing amiss." And then a dim dawning faith that this is no ordinary man. He is fainting in his pain. Death is drawing near, whatever death means, unconsciousness, nothingness, he does not know. From his dying soul goes forth that desperate cry, "Jesus, remember me when Thou comest in Thy kingdom!" And the heart of the Lord went out to him in a moment.

His parched lips can hardly form the words. But there is the majesty of a king in His reply to that dying man. "To-day thou shalt be with Me in Paradise!"

So came to the poor robber forgiveness and peace and a promise of life at the other side of death. For if the words meant anything they surely meant this: To-night, when our dead bodies are hanging on the Cross, you and I will be together in another world and we shall recognise each other there.

§ 4. *"Mother, Behold Thy Son"*

St. John xix. 25. The slow, torturing hours are passing. It is nearly noon. The sun is blazing hot and the holiday crowd are growing tired and scattering. Which gives room for the Blessed Virgin Mother and her two friends, attended by St. John, to draw near to the Cross. An awful sight for a mother. But no one shall hold her back. There is no comfort for her now but to be near Him, though she cannot even wipe His brow or cool His fevered lips. He is Messiah. He is her Lord. She does not forget that, though the mystery is yet beyond her. But just now above all else, He is her son, the infant who lay on her breast, the bright, brave Boy of the Nazareth workshop, the Youth who worked for her when Joseph died. It was awful for a mother. And in all His pain and all His great thoughts of the world's redemption and the glory to come, He is not too occupied to think of that widowed mother about to be doubly widowed now. Is it not "just like Him"? He looks lovingly on her and on that comrade who was so dear to Him. "Mother, behold thy son! Son, behold thy mother! And from that hour that disciple took her to his own home."

§ 5. Forsaken

St. Matthew xxvii. 45-48. Now comes sixth hour. What o'clock? Darkness lasted until? Dense darkness at noon-day. Must have frightened them all. Did they think He would come down from cross, as they mockingly asked? Darkness came as a veil to conceal His awful sufferings. Not merely of body. He could easily bear that. Awful torment of soul. We can't understand it. He knew it was coming on. He sent away His mother, to spare her the sight of it. No human being can ever understand the awful three hours' agony in the darkness on Calvary. He had looked forward to it with dread in the Garden of Gethsemane. We can judge of its awfulness by the awful cry at its close. What? (*v.* 46). What a tremendous impression that cry must have made. It is the *only one* of the words on the cross that either St. Matthew or St. Mark record.

We should read it: Why *didst* Thou? (See R. V. margin). He did not feel forsaken *now*. But he *had* in those awful three hours. It was over now but terrible to think of. "My God! My God! Why didst thou!"

We can dimly guess at the meaning of that cry. We are on holy ground at the most solemn point in the sufferings of our Lord. There seems but one way to understand it. That He was the Divine Sin-bearer, bearing the world's sin. "He was wounded for our transgressions, He was bruised," etc. (Isaiah liii. 5). God "made Him to be sin for us, Who knew no sin." The peculiar punishment of sin is the being abandoned by God. In some mysterious way our Lord had to be made to feel that—some sense of utter desolation—something so terrible that even He could hardly endure it. Yet it seemed necessary to the full bearing of our sin. We cannot understand it. But this we can understand, that it was all "for us men and for our salvation."

> "Yet once Immanuel's orphaned cry His universe
>   hath shaken;
>   It went up single, echoless, My God, I am forsaken!
>   It went up from His holy lips amid His lost creation
>   That no man else need ever cry that cry of desolation."

§ 6. *The End*

And now cometh the end. For all these hours He has been hanging upon the cross in awful conflict. Now, after that cry of agony, the conflict seems over, and the weary soul of the Redeemer turns to Heaven with that title of child-like love, which, through Him, ever since is permitted to us all. "It is finished," He said. "Father, into Thy hands," etc.; and, having said thus, He gave up the ghost.

Think of the loving words from the cross and the pleading of that love with the world to-day! How shall we escape if we neglect so great a salvation!

> "His tender voice pursues each one,
>   'My child, what more could thy God have done?
>   Thy sin hid the light of Heaven from Me:

When alone in the darkness I died for thee,
Thy sin of this day in its shadow lay
Between My face and God turned away."

"And we stop and turn for a moment's space
To fling back that love in the Saviour's face,
To give His heart yet another grief, and to glory
       in the wrong;
And still Christ keeps on loving us—loving all along."

Repeat at close the opening prayer: O Saviour of the World, etc.

QUESTIONS FOR LESSON XVIII

1. What different sets of people were around the Cross?

2. Mention the words from the Cross in order.

3. What things would the dying robber learn from Jesus' words?

4. Quote the awful saying about being forsaken.

5. What was the last saying?

THE RESURRECTION

HIS VISIT TO THE WORLD OF THE DEPARTED

St. Luke IX. 28-36 and XXIII. 39-43;

1. Peter III. 18 and IV. 6.

This is an unusual lesson in a Life of Christ. But I think it an important lesson, teaching of Death and of the Life Beyond. And it is certainly part of the life of Christ among men, though they are men passed out of this world. All through these lessons we have tried to keep the other world in view all the time. Our Lord always did so. Through all His teachings runs the thought of the other world encircling this world as the sea encircles the land. Everywhere the issues lead up to the world beyond. He sees us always in a wide, spacious universe where both worlds are one. And this lesson is intended to emphasise strongly that point of view.

§ 1. The World of the Departed

Last day we had the great, solemn story of our Lord dying on the Cross "for us men and for our salvation."

Remember His last words as He died? "Father, into Thy hands I commend My spirit." His spirit—His soul was going somewhere. Not yet into the final heaven. For He told them when He came back after the Resurrection: "I have not yet ascended to My Father."

He was going, as we all go when we die, into the great world of the Departed. Why don't we call it the World of the Dead? Think. Because they are not dead, they are more alive than we are—conscious and thinking and remembering and knowing and loving and remembering us as they always did. Jesus was constantly thinking of that world all around this world as the sea is around the land. In that world are all our dear ones who have died. There in the nearer presence of their Lord all the poor strugglers who have only begun to love Him on earth, will grow nearer to Him and learn to love Him better. They will be there to meet us when we go into that world at death, and surely they will have wonderful things to tell us. And one day will be a more glorious life for them when they reach the final heaven, where "Eye hath not seen nor ear heard, nor hath it entered into the heart of man to conceive the things that God has prepared for them that love Him."

Think of that wonderful world where our departed ones are living. What a wonderful, exciting thing it will be to die! To wake up after death as we awake in the morning after sleep and find ourselves there! And then to find our dear ones and hear what they have to tell us. And above all, if we have been humbly following our dear Lord on earth—to be in His closer presence there and learn how He cares for us and how much we have to thank Him for.

Surely it will be a wonderful thing to die. An old Indian officer one day was telling of his adventures, of his battles, of the Indian Mutiny, of the striking experiences of his life. His audience listened in breathless sympathy. At last he paused, and to their expressions of wonder he quietly replied: "I expect one day to see something much more wonderful." As he was a very old man they were greatly surprised. "I mean," said he, "in the first five minutes after death." That was how an old Christian man thought about that world of the departed. (Give pupils a chance here of talking and questioning.)

§ 2. Our Lord's Teaching

You remember how our Lord thought about that world? Remember in our last lesson. The dying robber is on a cross beside Him, just about to take his leap off into the dark. He does not know what death means, darkness, unconsciousness, nothingness, perhaps. He does not know. The only One who did know is beside him, and the poor, frightened soul turned to Him as he died, "Lord, remember me when Thou comest in Thy kingdom." And Jesus said: "To-day thou shalt be with me in paradise." Paradise was the Jewish word for the state of good men after death.

Surely He meant: "To-night, when our dead bodies are hanging on the cross, you and I will be together in the World of the Departed, and we shall remember each other as the two who hung on the cross this morning.

You remember at the Transfiguration (Luke ix. 28, etc.) the two men who had long been in that world and came out to talk to Him. Who? What did they talk of? Of his coming death in Jerusalem. Does it not suggest the interest which they and their comrades in that mysterious world were taking in their Lord's mission on earth? Can you imagine the joy to them when a few weeks later that Lord Himself, straight from the Cross, appeared in their world the triumphant victor, to visit the people who had never met Him on earth, to unfurl His banner and set up His cross in that World of the Departed. See what St. Peter writes in a letter about this. (Read 1. Peter iii. 18 and iv. 6, telling of His good news proclaimed to those departed souls). I think that St. Peter must have had some information to make him say that. Who only could have told him? The Lord himself. You remember in the Temptation when the Lord was quite alone yet all the disciples knew all about it. So the Lord must have told them. It was probably the same here, though the Bible does not tell us of His doing so. But how else could St. Peter know?

If only St. Peter knew we might not be sure. But St. Paul knew (Ephesians iv. 9). And what is much more convincing, we find just after the New Testament days, that the whole church knew that the Lord had gone on a wonderful visit to the World of the Dead, while His body lay in the grave.

§ 3. Teachings of the Early Church

About the time of St. John's death was born one Justin Martyr, a famous Christian writer. He writes very strongly about this visit of our Lord to the Unseen World.

A little later Irenæus, the famous bishop of Lyons in France, tells how the Lord entered the World of the Dead proclaiming His good news and that all who had hopes in Him receiving remission of sins.

Then away in Egypt, a great teacher called St. Clement of Alexandria, born about fifty years after St. John's death. We can read his writings now. He declares that the Lord preached His gospel to the dead and he thinks that the Apostles did the same when they died.

St. Clement had a well-known disciple, Origen. One day an infidel teacher named Celsus was laughing at him about this belief of the Church. "I suppose your Master, when He could not persuade the living, had to try if He could persuade the dead!" "Whether it please Celsus or not," said Origen, "we of the Church assert that the soul of our Lord did hold converse with other souls that He might convert those capable of instruction."

I love to see the enthusiasm of an old Bishop of Jerusalem, St. Cyril. He pictures the poor strugglers of old days and the patriarchs and prophets running to their Lord, crying in their delight: "O Death, where is thy sting? O Grave, where is thy victory? For the Conqueror hath redeemed us."

§ 4. *"He Descended into Hell"*

The strongest proof of this widespread belief is the statement in the Apostles' Creed, showing it as the belief of the whole church. Unfortunately we retain the old word hell, which is very misleading. The word should be Hades, the Unseen World. There is no thought in it of our Lord descending into what we call hell. See phrase in the Creed, "He descended into hell." We think of hell now only as a place of punishment. But the word had a much wider meaning when our Authorised Version of the Bible was prepared three hundred years ago and also when Creed was translated into English. Words often change in meaning, and we need to watch them. Three hundred years ago the word "hell" meant "the hole," "the unseen," "the covered-in and unknown world." "The World of the Departed after death." People believed that in it was a place of punishment—but much more that it was the unseen world of all the dead. Now you see how we need to guard against this mistake. When the Creed says, He descended into hell, what does it mean? What did it mean to the men who translated our Bible and to those who translated Creed into English? That he passed into the abode of the departed—into the World of the Dead. So our new Revised Bible has changed the word to "Hades" when it means the unseen world. Pity we don't change it in the Creed.

I think now you will see that there must be good grounds for all that widespread belief. Just think of the poor, desponding disciples giving up all hope when they saw their Lord dead. How little they knew the wonderful adventure on which He had gone and from which He came back on Easter morning!

QUESTIONS FOR LESSON XIX

1. What is the meaning of "He descended into hell?"

2. Why do you think it likely that our Lord visited the World of the Departed?

3. What did St. Peter say in his letter?

4. Tell me anything that other great men said.

5. How would such visit show Christ's love for men?

6. When did He return to earth from that wonderful world?

AN OLD MAN'S EASTER MEMORIES

St. John XIX. 38 to XX. 23.

(Extracts from the author's chapter, "An Old Man's Easter Memories," in his book, "A People's Life of Christ.")

We have been solemnly studying the death of our Lord and that wonderful visit to the World of the Departed which the disciples at the time knew nothing about. Now return back to earth again to see these poor disciples in their desolate sorrow, that you may realise better the glad, overwhelming surprise of the Easter morning. Make pictures in your minds as we go on.

§ 1. Friday Night

A funeral in a beautiful garden, amid the brightness and perfume of flowers, in the quiet sunset time. Oh! what a miserable funeral! Did ever such hopeless mourners follow a corpse as those who followed the blood-stained body of Jesus to the tomb that evening? Did ever such desolate hearts return from a funeral?

It is a terrible, dismal thing returning from any funeral—leaving body of loved one in grave—going into empty house—thinking of all the long, dreary days of loneliness stretching out in front. All that here. But far worse. Not only lost the dearest, truest friend, but lost all the bright hopes of the future. They had thought He was the Divine Messiah—to redeem Israel—to found the Kingdom of God—to dwell with them always in power and glory. What an awful disappointment and shaking of their trust to see Him arrested and tried like a common prisoner—helpless in the power of His enemies, mocked and scourged, and spat upon; nailed upon a cross between two common robbers; taunted to come down, and not doing so; bleeding and weakening, and at last dying like any ordinary man; the pale, blood-stained corpse put into the tomb. Surely there is an end of all—their love, their hopes, their future are all buried in the tomb. He could not be the Christ of God, after all. He must have been mistaken. He was good and pure and holy. The noblest heart that ever came from God. But could He have been the Son of God, since death had conquered Him? Thus they went home from that funeral with hearts utterly crushed. Two of them were too heart-broken to go home at all. Who? Think of the two solitary women sitting there alone as the dark night fell on them, in their passionate, despairing grief, in the deep, hopeless love. That is our last view we get of the funeral of Jesus.

§ 2. Saturday

The Sabbath day, when people rested from their work and went to church to worship God. Oh the misery and desolation of that Sabbath! Judas hanged. Peter crushed with remorse; all the rest sunk in hopeless grief; going to church, perhaps; hearing the prayers said by the cruel priests who had murdered their friend; then the men planning sadly to go back to their fishing, and the women waiting through the night with spices and ointments—for what? Keep body from corruption. How utterly blind to the great joy before them!

§ 3. An Old Man's Easter Memories[3]

I advise teachers to read the rest of this chapter for the class just as it stands.

Then came the glad, overwhelming surprise of the Easter morning. I am not going to describe it. I should probably spoil the story. And I am not going over the separate long accounts in St. Matthew, St. Mark, and St. Luke. That would only tire you. I am going to take you away to a little church in Ephesus fifty years afterwards and let you listen to a very old white-haired man telling his memories of that glad day when he was young.

St. John wrote his gospel very many years after the other gospels. He was then an old man, living far away from the scenes of his youth. The young peasant of the

---

[3]I advise teachers to read the rest of this chapter for the class just as it stands.

164

Lake of Galilee was now the beloved bishop of the church of Ephesus. But the old man's eyes are ever turning back to the past—to those three wonderful years when he walked the fields of Palestine with Jesus—"the disciple whom Jesus loved." How wonderful were those years, looking back on them through the golden haze of the Resurrection and Ascension, "when," as he says, "we beheld His glory, the glory of the only begotten of the Father full of grace and truth" (John i. 14).

The old comrades were gone. James and Peter and Andrew and Philip were long ago departed to be with their Master in the Unseen, and he was left alone of all that band, brooding as an old man will, on the precious memories of the past.

> I'm growing very old. This weary head
> That hath so often leaned on Jesus' breast
> In days long past that seem almost a dream,
> Is bent and hoary with its weight of years.
> I'm old—so old I cannot recollect
> The faces that I meet in daily life;
> But that dear Face and every word He spake
> Grow more distinct as others fade away,
> So that I live with Him and the holy dead
> More than the living.

And how his people loved to hear the old man's memories of those years! They had probably some of the other gospels in writing. But it was so different to hear their dear old bishop tell what he remembered—and he remembered so many things not written in their books. Year after year, he told them what he knew and as he told it repeatedly the story grew into shape and

so there came to us the Gospel of St. John, THE GOSPEL
OF AN OLD MAN'S MEMORIES.

§ 4. *The Napkin and the Grave Clothes*

In this gospel of his memories he does not tell of
the Resurrection itself. He is recalling the day when into
his despair and desolation crept the first dawning belief
that the dear Lord was back with them, alive.

Something happened that forced immediate
conviction. "Then I saw and believed," he says
(*ch. xx. 8*).

"Master, tell us," they would say, "what did you see?
Why did you believe?"

"I will tell you. It was this way. On the first day of the
week, Mary Magdalene went early to the tomb while
it was yet dark. She saw the stone rolled away and the
tomb empty! She thought the body had been stolen.
Terrified, she rushed back to our lodging to tell Peter
and me. We ran full speed to see. I was the younger. I
got there first and I looked into the tomb and saw it was
as Mary had said. But I went not in. Then as I looked,
Peter arrived and went straight in, and I watched him
beholding, gazing, staring at the empty grave clothes
and the napkin rolled up away by itself: Something
about them evidently astonished him.

Then I went in, and when I saw what Peter was
staring at—*then I saw and believed!*"

Now what do you think forced his instant belief?
The empty grave clothes alone would not absolutely

make him believe any more than they made Mary believe. The body might have been stolen away. Why did Peter stare so at the appearance of the winding sheet and the napkin? And why did John, when he saw what Peter was staring at, immediately believe?

Sixteen years ago, Dr. Latham, a well-known scholar in an English university, was in the East. While visiting a cemetery he saw several funeral processions come in. The bodies were carried on biers. They all lay face upwards. The grave clothes were all alike. The face, neck, and upper surface of the shoulders were in every case uncovered, so that between the grave clothes and the napkin that enveloped the top of the head, a space of a foot or more, the body was wholly bare.

Remembering how slowly customs change in the East, and how especially slowly burial customs change everywhere, we may safely assume that this was how Jesus' body was dressed.

Now picture to yourselves that dead body, laid in the tomb, the winding sheet reaching up to the shoulders and the napkin around the crown of the head. Then picture the appearance of the winding sheet and napkin, supposing the body had turned to dust, or turned to air, or vanished or exhaled or spiritualized *without disturbing the wrappings.*

Now follow Peter as he went into the tomb. At once he saw that something most unusual had happened. The linen clothes were not torn open or folded up on the shelf. They were lying unmoved as if the body were still in them except that they had fallen flat, for the body had gone out of them but had not displaced them. Moreover, he saw that the napkin around the head was lying undisturbed on its raised step by itself still with its "roll" in it as at the funeral, only it had fallen a little flat, for the head had gone out of it, but otherwise it was undisturbed. It was a "rolled-round napkin," St. John says.

All this arrested Peter's eye. John looked in and only "sees," but Peter when he went in and was arrested by this remarkable phenomenon "beholds," stares at the clothes as they lie, and the rolled-round napkin unchanged in its place by itself as when the body was laid there. If he had seen that the linen clothes had been unwrapped from the body and folded up and laid on the ledge and that the same had been done to the napkin, he would have only known that the body had gone and he saw that in any case. He might have hoped that Jesus had risen but he could not feel absolutely sure. Any hands might have unwound the clothes and folded them. But from what he saw, it was clear that no hands had been there at all. The body had simply moved out, exhaled itself from the clothes without disturbing them or loosing their fastenings and the clothes had fallen flat—the head simply moved out of the napkin without disturbing it and then also it had fallen a little flat. It seemed plain that no one had removed the body, it had actually risen. No man's hand had done it, it had been done by the mighty power of God.

Then went in also that other disciple (John), who came first to the sepulchre, and he says immediately, *"I saw and believed!"* To see the body gone was not to believe with certainty. But to see that the body had gone out of its wrappings without disturbing them though they had been wound round and round, and that the head had gone out of the napkin, leaving it still "wound round" and that hundred-pound weight of spices lay still in the clothes, this was to believe that Jesus must have risen from the dead.

Now have you pictured all this, and got it quite clear? You see why St. John says, "Then I saw and believed"?

§ 5. *The Excitement of Easter Morning*

Thus the old man told of the first startled dawning of hope on that Easter morning fifty years before. But I can imagine the people asking, "Is that all?"

"All! Why, no. I am only telling of my first conviction that the Lord was risen. After that, we saw Him over and over again. Sometimes I was present. Sometimes I was not."

"But, Master, tell us your own personal memories of that time."

"I remember that morning after Peter and I got back to the others. We were eagerly trying to tell what we had seen when again Mary Magdalene burst in, all trembling and excited. 'Oh, I have seen the Lord!' she cried, 'actually seen Him! He has spoken to me! He bade me come and tell you! I did not recognise Him at first. I was frightened at the empty tomb. I thought the body had been taken away and I thought it was the gardener who might tell me about it. Then He just looked at me for a moment! And my heart stood still! And then—He just called my name in the old, familiar tones: "Mary!" And I knew! I knew! I fell down at His feet and cried, Rabboni! Rabboni! And he bade me come and tell you all!'

"That evening we were all together again. We had fastened the doors, through fear of the Jews. We were talking and wondering and tremblingly hoping—we hardly knew what. Some of the women had told us of angels at the tomb, but we did not believe them. We thought that even Mary's story might be just an excited fancy. But Peter had just come in with a strange new look in his eyes, and he told us positively that the Lord had appeared and spoken to him. He would not talk about it. He has never talked about it since. But he was sure—sure. We were greatly excited. The excitement was so intense that even when two disciples from the Emmaus road burst in with fresh tidings, they could not get a chance to speak for the cries of delight that met them. 'The Lord is risen! The Lord is risen! He has appeared to Simon Peter!' When they got a chance, they told us how He had met them and walked and talked with them and was known to them in the breaking of bread.[4]

"So we listened and wondered and hoped and rejoiced. Then—suddenly—a solemn silence fell—JESUS WAS PRESENT! No one had heard Him come. No one

[4]St. John does not put this incident in his record, probably because it was already written in St. Luke's gospel. But it evidently belongs to this meeting, where he was present, and would most probably be related in these reminiscences to his people.

had unbarred the door—but He was there! We were frightened. We thought it was His ghost. But He looked on us in the old way and spake in His own voice. We heard His old familiar greeting, 'Peace be unto you!' and we could doubt no longer. It was no ghost. It was Himself in radiant bodily form. Then He breathed on us and said: 'Receive the Holy Ghost. As my Father hath sent me, so I send you.' And oh! we disciples were glad when we saw the Lord.

"I remember when we told Thomas that night and he would not believe us. 'It is impossible,' he said; 'you must be mistaken. Except I shall see the wounds and the print of the nails, I will not believe.'

"All that week we went about dazed, like men in a dream. Then the following Sunday the Lord came to us again. We never knew when He would come or from whence. This time Thomas was with us. And I shall never forget how He talked with Thomas and showed him His wounded hands and feet, and how Thomas was so astonished and so broken with joy that he could only fall at His feet in adoration and cry: 'My Lord and my God!'

§ 6. By the Lakeside

"Ah, yes. We saw Him many other times during the Forty Days. One of these times is specially in my mind, and Peter never forgot it to the end of his life. We had all been bidden by the Lord to meet Him in Galilee. We were back in the homeland, back near Capernaum, by the lakeside with all its memories of the old happy days together. While we waited for His promised coming to the mountain, we had a wonderful experience. We had been out all night fishing in Peter's boat—Peter and my brother James and I and Thomas and Nathaniel and two others. We had no success. All night we toiled and rowed and flung the nets, but we caught nothing, just as on that other day three years before, when He first called us. Just as the day was breaking, we saw Him on the shore. Oh, I knew, I felt sure that it was He. But I could not speak. The others did not know Him in the dim dawn.

"Then we heard a voice clearly across the water: 'My children, cast your net on the right side of the boat and ye shall find.' They cast the net wearily without much hope. But the moment they tried to pull it in, a great wonder and dread fell on them. They could not pull it in, it was so heavy with fishes. Then I could not keep quiet any longer. 'Oh,' I cried, 'it is the Lord! it is the Lord!' And Peter flung himself straight into the sea, for we were near the land, and we all hurried into the little boat and hastened after him. And there was Jesus Himself on the shore, Jesus my Lord and my God!

"Then three times he asked Peter, 'Lovest thou Me?' and three times recommissioned him, 'Feed my sheep. Feed my lambs.' And He said a strange thing about me that I don't understand. Peter asked Him, 'What shall John do?' And He said, 'If I will that John tarry till I come what is that to thee?' I don't know what that meant."

"Master, do you think He meant that you should not die at all?"

"Ah, I don't know. I have lived so long now. They are all gone but me. Some think that He meant that. But He did not say that."

These are only some of St. John's personal memories. Others told of other meetings with the risen Lord. But these memories of the aged disciple help us to realise the wonder and joy and delightful excitement of the first Easter Day.

QUESTIONS FOR LESSON XX

1. Did the disciples expect the Resurrection?

2. What was their attitude on Friday evening and Saturday?

3. Who first knew of Resurrection?

4. Tell St. John's story of the napkin and grave clothes.

5. Explain exactly what convinced Peter and John.

6. Tell St. John's further memories of Easter Day.

LESSON XXI

LESSONS OF EASTER DAY

St. Matthew XXVIII.; St. Mark XVI. 1.

I am giving two lessons on the Resurrection
(1) Because it is so important a subject that it should
be fully impressed on pupils; (2) Because it introduces
another scripture than that in last lesson; (3) Because
last lesson was only narrative, and this one emphasises
the teachings of Easter; (4) If thought advisable, this
lesson can be omitted here and kept as a special lesson
for Easter Day.

§ 1. Easter Morning

Read St. Matthew xxviii. Who had been latest at the
grave on Friday night? Who first at tomb on the Sunday?
Somehow it seems that their love and devotion were
deeper than that of the men. I think it is so generally.
Perhaps, because women are to be the mothers of
the race, and to bring up the little children, God has
given them in a very high measure the grace of fidelity
and devotion. And the Lord Jesus seems to have had
especially the power of drawing it out. In His whole

174

life we never hear of any woman being hostile to Him. Perhaps it was the self-sacrifice in Him that touched and attracted them. Do you think they had more faith and hope than the men? Did they expect the Lord to rise? How do you know they did not? What did they bring to the tomb? (See Mark xvi. 1). Yes; to preserve the body from decay. You see they, too, had lost faith, and lost hope; but what had they not lost? Love. Their love, stronger than death, kept them watching at the tomb after all the others; brought them early to the tomb before all others. And so the highest honour was given to them. It was a woman who first saw the Lord after He arose. Who? It was women who first received His loving salutation. And even since, through His influence, the whole position of woman in the world has been changed. Wherever Christianity has power, woman is no longer despised and degraded, as in the olden days, but honoured and treated with chivalrous courtesy, according to the will of Christ.

St. Mark (xvi.) says there were three women. Perhaps the Magdalene had moved away or gone around another path. St. John's memory of her hardly fits in here. (See last lesson.)

Now think of the two women walking sorrowfully up the Calvary path to anoint a dead body. And then think of their sudden and awful terror—think of the earthquake shaking the hills—of the burst of terrific glory and the diamond-shining whiteness of the angel's wings. For I think the women saw it all, probably in the distance. St. Matthew uses the word "Behold!" (*v.* 2), as if to suggest the start that it gave them. St. Luke tells of two angels. St. Matthew of but one, perhaps because that one was the speaker. But whether one or two, we may be sure that the sight made the women's hearts beat fast with expectation. Surely, surely, angels would not come but for some great purpose!

How glad the angels must have been to have such joyful news—to be the heralds of the King again. Do you remember first time they were His heralds? Christmas hymn, "Hark! the herald," etc. Perhaps these same two had been in that Christmas chorus at Bethlehem. Do you remember other times that they were attending the Lord on earth? The Temptation, the Agony, the Ascension. Don't you think they were glad at Easter? And with no selfish gladness. For they had no fear of death themselves. But glad for the poor, sorrowful world; and glad, with wondering gladness, for themselves, at the further knowledge of the Divine love.

What was the announcement to women? How did they receive it? Fear and great joy. Too frightened and astonished to grasp the glad news at first. But oh! what delight as soon as they realised it. Not only their Lord alive, but all their old trust and hope restored. He *was* the Christ, the Son of God, after all. He had not deceived them or been mistaken. All that He had said about Heaven and immortality was true—grandly, gloriously true. What a glad, delightful change from the misery of yesterday!

That whole Easter day was so full of rumours and excitement and wild astonishment and delight that it is hard to arrange events in order.

176

Now run over the events in St. John's memories in last lesson—add the events here. Try to put eight or nine in order for me of the happenings of that Easter Day.

§ 2. Resurrection Shews Us That Jesus Was God

Why did the disciples believe in the Resurrection? Because they saw it, and were thoroughly convinced of it. Why do you believe that I am teaching this class to-day? Have you any doubt about it? Apostles felt like that. Mary saw Him—and Peter—and the men at Emmaus, and the eleven disciples—and Thomas—and the 500 brethren, etc. Were they glad?

Have *we* any reason to be glad about it? Would it matter to us if story not true, if disciples really stole away the body while soldiers slept? Why should it matter to us? Now think.

(1) MAKES US SURE THAT JESUS WAS GOD.— Resurrection most important proof of this. One had come on earth not to be distinguished in appearance from other men. But He said that He was God. That He had come down to die for men—that through His death there was forgiveness of sins—that if a man believed in Him, though he were dead, yet should he live, etc. And people said:—"This would be blessed news if true, but it is not." "Ay, but it is true," said the Apostles, and "God has proved it in that He raised Him from the dead."

This the Apostles especially insisted on. They pledged the very existence of Christianity to the truth of it. "If Christ be not risen, then is our preaching vain, and your faith is also vain." (See 1 Corinthians xv. 12-19.) In the Acts of the Apostles we find it was the main subject of their preaching, and the main thought about themselves was as "witnesses of the Resurrection." (Teacher here read rapidly Acts i. 8, 21, 22; iii. 15; iv. 2, 33; xvii. 18; xxiv. 21, etc.) "We are sure of it," they said. "We are witnesses. We twelve men saw Jesus of Nazareth. Some of us lived near Him as boys. We lived with Him as men. We saw Him work miracles; saw Him arrested, tried, crucified, dead. And then we saw Him risen again—and if you don't believe us, ask the 500 brethren and the others who saw Him. We are sure, positively and certainly. Therefore we know that Christ is God, and that we may depend on all that He told us of His power and glory, and the heaven by and by."

And because they were so sure they could bear everything—trouble, torture, imprisonment. "We don't care," they said: "the Lord Jesus is risen—gone up to heaven. He sees it all. We are only glad to bear anything or do anything for Him."

§ 3. Shews Us That We Shall Live Again

Now see another reason why we should be glad about Easter. It tells of our life after death. What an enormous difference that would make in this poor world of sorrow and death! Think of the world before Christ—and the poor heathen world to-day. Think of poor mother breaking her heart over her dead child. Tell you of funeral 2,000 years ago. A girl, daughter of a great wise Roman named Cicero—beautiful procession—people standing silent around—mother sobbing—father pale and stern, but too proud to cry over his dead child.

No one to comfort him but one old friend named Sulpicius, who had written him a letter of comfort. Poor old man, it was the best comfort that he could give. Should you like to hear it? "Don't fret," he said; "everybody must die—it is only a girl—remember that you are the great wise Cicero. You should, therefore, have great fortitude. You should be too proud to cry over your dead child." That was all the comfort he could give. What a miserable comfort! Then came the priests in their stately robes, to sing the sad burial words at the tomb. Guess what they sang? "There will be no parting there"? "Safe in the Arms of Jesus"? Oh! no. This is their hymn: "Vale, vale, in aeternum vale," *i.e.,* "Farewell, farewell, for ever and ever, farewell!" Alas for the poor sorrowing pagan world who did not know of Christ and Easter. What a glad thing for us who do! How we should rejoice and thank God!

§ 4. The Easter Missionary Message

When their hearts were so full of the glad news, what directions did they get? (*v.* 7). What missionary thought does that suggest to us? That the new glad knowledge brought with it a new glad duty to go off at once and make others sharers in the joy. It was a "day of good tidings"; they must not hold their peace.

As they started on their errand, what happened? (Matthew xxviii. 9). Don't you think they were glad?

And as they fall at His feet in loving reverent worship, is there not something about our Missionary Lesson again? Ah, yes. "Go and tell my brethren." Worship is good. The joy of lying at His feet is good; but better, and more acceptable in His sight, to go off and tell the good news to those who do not yet know it. So the lesson for us, too. Think of the poor heathen who don't know that glad message at all. When their little children die, they do not hope to meet them again. When they are dying themselves, they know nothing of the blessed hereafter, nor of the great love of God, revealed through Jesus Christ. What should we be able to tell the poor, heathen mother about Easter to make her heart glad? (1) That we know Jesus Christ was God, He who took the children in His arms; and therefore we know God's feelings towards the children. (2) That He promised that there should be an eternal life after death and proved it by rising Himself after death. (3) That, therefore, a poor mother can with fearless heart, commit her dying child to Him who loved the little children. Death is now for us but the threshold of the great glad eternal life. The dying child is but as the dying caterpillar on the leaf, who shall by and by burst its withered shell and soar out in the sunshine. "Them also that sleep in Jesus will God bring with Him; wherefore comfort one another with these words" (1 Thessalonians iv. 14, 18). Do you think the Easter news worth having? Is it worth telling? When your church asks for prayers and for money to help missions remember that. It means looking after the interests of Jesus. It means telling to poor, sorrowful heathen, news that is worth while. Will some of you pray that, if it be God's will, He will let you go out, when you grow up, to teach the poor heathen the glad message about our Lord? It is so hard to get people to go.

QUESTIONS FOR LESSON XXI

1. Give five instances of the angels attending on our Lord on earth.

2. Two reasons why we to-day should be glad about the Easter story.

3. Tell about death and funeral of Cicero's child.

4. Reasons for taking interest in missionary work?

5. Further reason at Ascension? Matthew xxviii. 19.

LESSON XXII

THE GREAT FORTY DAYS

Acts I, 1-5; 1 Corinthians XV. 3-9.

The main thought in this lesson is the impression left on the disciples that the Lord was with them all the time, invisible, watching over them and thinking of them. For forty days He stayed on earth unseen—now and then, suddenly, unexpectedly, presenting Himself to them—so that they felt Him near all the time, though they could not see Him, and thus they gradually learned to think of Him as "with them always even to the end of the world" so that they could think of Him as near—and speak to Him and pray to Him—feeling Him in close touch with them. They would of course *believe* His word that He could be with them and hear their prayers, etc., but it would be harder to *feel and realise it* if it were not for this lesson of the Forty Days. Teachers might say something of this to pupils as an Introduction.

§ 1. *The Two Great Lessons*

Did the Lord disappear from sight into heaven immediately after the Easter appearances? How long

182

after Easter day did He stay with them? Did He live with them constantly and familiarly like the Comrade that He was in earthly life? No. That would only have made them think of Him as like Lazarus raised from the dead to the old, ordinary human life. That was not what happened at all. That would not have so clearly shown that He was God nor helped them to realise how He could be invisibly present with His people always in every part of the world. You see, there were two things to be taught:

(1) To show the reality of the Resurrection—that "this same Jesus," their beloved Master and Comrade, had risen from the dead. That was easy enough to learn. The delight of that first Easter day settled that the Lord is risen, the beloved Comrade and Friend is back with us. He whom we saw dead is alive again. He whom we trusted to redeem Israel has not failed us after all. Oh, the delight of that when they had utterly lost heart and brought spices to keep His dead body from decay, the delight of finding that He was alive, that He had conquered death and come back as victor into the midst of them again. That was easy to learn.

(2) But that was not all. They must learn that this was no rising to ordinary human life like Lazarus, that this was a new, mysterious, glorified life to which their Lord had risen. They had to feel the deep conviction that He was God. They had to be taught to realise how He could be with them always, even when unseen. These were some of the things they had to be taught by these Forty Days.

§ 2. How Second Lesson Began

The first of these lessons we have been learning in the Easter story. To-day we deal with the second.

Now see how this second lesson was taught. They saw at once with awe and wonder how different this was from the poor human life of the risen Lazarus. They found Him for forty days invisible, living near and close to them. As the forty days went by the awe and wonder deepened. They see Him no longer subject to human needs nor bound by the natural laws of earth. How tired He used to be—and hungry and thirsty—how glad He was of the rest and shelter of the Bethany home! All this is changed. The risen Lord needs neither shelter nor rest nor food. Forty days He lingers in the world but in no earthly home. Steadily the conviction grew that the Lord was moving in another and higher sphere of existence than that of the old days on earth. That would give such a solemn feeling about Him. So their lesson was begun.

§ 3. His Appearances

Then came His appearances and repeated intercourse with them during these days. They felt He was near them all the time unseen. Then suddenly He would make Himself visible and then vanish, become invisible though they knew He was not gone away from them. He is seen and recognised only as He wills, and when He wills. He appears suddenly and is not seen coming. He appears unexpectedly and as suddenly disappears. He comes to them through doors that are barred and fastened. He arranges to meet them in Galilee but does not go with them. When they are there He suddenly appears. He speaks to Thomas words that show that He was present and listening unknown to them when Thomas expressed his doubt. Thus the conviction of His unseen presence would gradually grow on them. They were learning their lesson.

I think He must have appeared more times than are recorded. How many times do you remember? Could you remember ten or eleven? (1) To Mary Magdalene (St. John xx. 1); (2) to Peter (Luke xxiv. 34); (3) to the Emmaus travellers (Luke xxiv. 13); (4) to the assembled apostles without Thomas (John xx. 19); (5) the following Sunday when Thomas was with them (John xx. 26); (6) by the Lake of Galilee (John xxi.) Then St. Paul tells of some more: (7) To the 500 in Galilee (1 Corinthians xv. 6); (8) to James (1 Corinthians xv. 7); (9) to the eleven at Jerusalem (Luke xxiv. 44); (10) at the Ascension. Probably more, not recorded. When He taught them concerning the Kingdom of God which they were to establish on earth (Acts i. 3). I should suppose, too, that He appeared to His mother. But we don't know.

§ 4. What These Appearances Taught

Now look at a few of these. Mary Magdalene in her joyful astonishment throws herself at His feet. "Rabboni! My Master!" She has found the Friend whom she had lost, but no more. She has no loftier title than the old one. My Master! My Teacher! He is to her the same human Jesus. His resurrection is a return to the old life. She would clasp His feet with loving hands. Therefore in His reply He corrects and raises her thought. "Touch me not, Mary. Don't take hold of me. Don't cling to me. Things are changed. But go and tell my brethren to meet me." It was the first indication that the old intimacy is to be changed for a higher fellowship.

Then with the disciples on Emmaus road (Luke xxiv. 13). As soon as they had clearly recognised Him, He vanished from sight, and so the truth dawned on them that He now belonged to new order, that the claims of the invisible world were on Him, a world into which they could not follow Him yet.

Then He appears in the midst to the assembled disciples (John xx. 19), suddenly, unexpectedly, "when the doors were shut" and barred. Doors and bars were no obstacle to Him. At first they thought it was His ghost. No. It was He himself in radiant bodily form, speaking the old kindly salute, Peace be unto you—"this same Jesus," but mysteriously changed. And so through all the other appearances. With awe and reverence and wonder, they saw Him affectionately near but far above them.

He was different yet the same. He retained the little peculiarities of voice and manner and gesture which distinguish one man from another. And His love to them was unchanged, as in the old days. And the old themes of conversation were quietly resumed as if death and these three days had not intervened at all. "Tell my brethren to go back to Galilee as I told you (before I died)." Wait in Jerusalem for the promised Holy Ghost of whom ye heard from me (before I died). The continuity was unbroken between the old life and the new.

And He continued His treatment and training of them as before. We remember His training of Peter in the old days. Now it goes on in similar way. That loving message to Peter through the angels at the tomb: "Tell my disciples and especially tell Peter, who is breaking his heart over his shameful denial. Don't leave Peter out." Then that meeting by the lakeside (John xxi. 7). And so, too, with Thomas and the rest.

§ 5. With Them Always

Then notice the change in their attitude towards Him. They used to sit and talk and eat with Him in familiar intercourse. One would lean on His breast at supper, etc. Now all this intimacy is over. They are adoring Him, worshipping Him, speaking of Him with awe as my Lord and my God!

Gradually but surely, they learned the lesson of the Forty Days that it was the Eternal Son of God in disguise who had been their Comrade and Friend—that He had passed into a higher order—that He could be present with them though they saw Him not, that a spiritual and eternal fellowship was to take the place of the old temporal and visible comradeship of the Galilee days.

What do you think was the strongest proof that

they had learned the lesson that He would be always with them? I think their joy after the Ascension (Luke xxiv. 52). Why? Because at such parting we might surely expect sorrow and desolation, that earth would be a poor, lonely place without Him. Should not you expect that? But no. After that parting "they returned to Jerusalem *with great joy!*" (John xxiv. 52). Surely they had learned the lesson of the Forty Days that He would be with them and near them always to the end of the world. And so that lesson has come down to us. Jesus is not far off but near us always. We can enter into our closet and shut to the door, and there on our knees talk to Him and feel close to Him.

§ 6. Our Dear Ones in the Unseen

Don't you think, too, that His intercourse with His disciples after His death should make us feel hopeful about the attitude of our dear ones after their death. The Forty Days tell us of Him who was dead like our dead once; who went through the dark river as they did and reached the further shore; yet when He came back to meet His friends on earth He was as affectionate and as much their own as ever. The river of death had not washed out the memory of the old days nor the affection for the old friends. Of course He was God and so was different from our dead, but they are with Him in that unseen world now, and are learning love more than ever before. So we feel that we shall know them as the disciples knew the Lord and we cannot help hoping very delightful things when we meet them again. And this adds another to the many things for which we have to thank our dear Lord. We are going to have a very lovely time some day in the future.

QUESTIONS FOR LESSON XXII

1. What were the two things to be taught to the disciples by the Resurrection and the Forty Days?

2. Which of these was hardest to learn? Why?

3. How many appearances of the Lord can you remember?

4. Show how any of these appearances helped to teach the second of the two lessons mentioned?

5. Tell me a good proof that the disciples had learned it.

6. Do the Forty Days help us to hope some pleasant things about our departed friends? How?

THE ASCENSION

LESSON XXIII

THE ASCENSION

Read (1) St. Luke XXIV. 44 to end;

(2) St. Mark XVI. 19 to end;

(3) Acts I. 8-12.

§ 1. End of His Visit to Earth

Now we come to the close of the Lord's visit to earth. We have just learned of the most solemn and wonderful events of His life. The Crucifixion, the Resurrection, the great Forty Days. Now it is quite clear that something else great and solemn must happen. What? The Ascension. Why? Because, if the Lord did not go back into heaven, then He must be here in bodily presence still, which He is not, or He must have grown old and weak and died again, like any ordinary man, which would be a very poor ending for His wonderful life. Therefore we are quite prepared to hear of Ascension. We should be quite puzzled at the whole story of Christ if no Ascension.

You see, this visit to earth in human form was only one little incident, one little episode, of thirty years in

His eternal life. This "Story of the Gospels" is only one tiny bit of "the Life of Christ for men." So when He came from Heaven at Christmas, He was to go back again when His mission was accomplished. You see how very simply He puts it Himself. "I came forth from the Father and came into this world. Now I leave the world and go back to the Father" (John xvii. 28). Don't you think the angels who sang "the glad tidings" of Christmas night when He came to us would be eagerly looking forward now to His return?

§ 2. His Good-bye

So one day came the last interview of that wonderful Forty Days. He was teaching His last lesson of the "things concerning the Kingdom of God," reminding them of what had happened, telling them, "Ye are to be my witnesses to tell the world these things." He was entrusting the world to them! I should think they would feel proud and touched at His trust in them and ashamed that they so little deserved it and surely frightened at this tremendous task that He set them. But they must not be frightened. He would be with them more than ever, watching over and helping them. "All power has been given to me in heaven and on earth. Go ye therefore and make disciples of all the nations, baptising them into the name of the Father, and of the Son, and of the Holy Ghost, teaching them to observe all things whatsoever I have commanded you, and lo! I am with you always even to the end of the world."

Keep this in mind always when you are asked

to pray and give money for missions to the heathen. Remember it was your dear Lord's last wish before He went away.

§ 3. Returning to the Father

Then He led them out as far as Bethany for His last good-bye. Picture that walk. A little band of twelve men moving through suburbs of Jerusalem to the Bethany road over the lower slopes of Mount of Olives. Ever been on that road before? Tell me of any occasions? Yes. Very tender associations. He had often walked wearily there, looking forward to friendly greeting in somebody's house at Bethany. Whose? There the disciples had gone with Him when Lazarus was raised. They would remember that now. But more solemn and sad memories. They cross over Kedron again. When before? They walk near Gethsemane, where He had struggled in His awful agony, and where they all forsook Him and fled. What a strange walk, never to be forgotten, would be this last walk with the Lord! What a remembrance in after days that good-bye would be! There He stood in His mysterious Resurrection body, listening patiently to their questions about the times and the seasons, and directing them about their great missionary work "to the uttermost part of the earth." There the most wonderful thing in the world's history was about to take place. Did the world take any notice? No. Not even Jerusalem, which lay so near. Herod and Pontius Pilate and the priests and the busy merchants were all about their own work and took no

195

notice. Angels would be watching eagerly for the return of the Lord to Heaven, but the world then, as now, did not trouble much about Him.

Ah! the world had not been kind to Him! He had lived a life that seemed so certain to win love; but they would not love Him, they preferred a murderer to Him. Even the little group who stood round Him now to say good-bye—had they been kind to Him? Peter who denied—Thomas who doubted—the rest who forsook Him. But did He remember and remind them of their faults just now? Ah, no! The cross and the desertion and the ingratitude had not embittered Him in the least. In loving, tender farewell He lifted up His hands and blessed them. And while He blessed them what happened? (Luke xxiv. 51). Is it not a pleasant thought, the last sight men ever saw of Christ was while His lips were uttering words of love and His hands were stretched out in blessing? Did you ever go to see off at boat or train some relative or close friend? Would you not remember how they looked when saying good-bye? Always think about the last view of the Lord saying good-bye. It was "just like Him," as we say. Just like all His life of kindness and love.

Did they see Him go up into heaven? What hindered? (Acts i. 9). They could not see up. Could He still see down? Do you think He was still blessing? So to-day that cloud between us. Can we see Him? Can He see us? Do you think He cares what we are doing? Do you think He is blessing us still?

How startled the Apostles were—staring up

wonderingly, longingly. Perhaps they wanted to go, too, or wanted Him to come back to them. Who spoke to them? Perhaps the two angels that had been in tomb. Perhaps "two men," Moses and Elias, who in shining apparel had come to Him before. When? (Mark ix. 4). What did they say? Was it wrong to be looking—longing after Christ? No; better if we looked and longed more. Why blame them? Because Christ had left them plenty of work to do for Him, and they were to go and busy themselves about it (*v.* 8), and not be merely sentimentalizing. What was the promise they gave? When shall He so come? Second Advent. In like manner—what manner? Blessing His people. He went away to heaven blessing His disciples, and He will come back blessing them. And meantime? Still blessing. Do we look forward to this coming? A father left his boy in a great crush at East India House, promising to come back for him. In the hurry of business he forgot him until evening. Rushed back in great fright. Boy standing wearily where he had left him. "I knew you would come back, father; you said you would."

Will His coming be a joy and blessing to everybody? Why not? What an awful thing if we missed His blessing. "We believe that Thou shalt come to be our Judge; we therefore pray Thee, help Thy servants whom Thou hast redeemed with Thy precious blood."

§ 4. A New "Life of Christ"

Have we now finished with the "Life of Christ for men"? Surely not. Never think of Jesus as gone away.

197

He is closer to us than ever. He is still watching over us, thinking for us, caring for us and, better still, "He ever liveth to make intercession for us" (Hebrews vii. 25). Our Friend, our brother, our dear Master who loves us and for ever is watching over our interests in heaven. "The Life of Christ for men," is still going on. Do you think there will ever be written any further "Life of Christ"? I do think it. The great souls of earth gone into that world will surely write chapters of that "Life of Christ for men" continued after He had returned from earth. And I think one of the wonderful experiences for us after we die will be reading of that continued Life and loving Him for it more than we have ever loved Him here. Some very wonderful experiences are waiting us in that Other World.

§ 5. *Gifts unto Men*

But we can only study at present the Life of Christ on earth that we know.

Now think what the Ascension has gained for us. Here is the great Victor, the fierce conflict over, going to receive His crown. Ancient victors in their processions scattered gifts among the crowd. So the Lord, victorious now. How pleasant to Him to think of how He had borne the Temptation, the Agony, the Cross, all for men. So shall we feel whenever we have conquered temptation for His sake. Now the resistless Victor returning to be crowned. "Highly exalted and given a name above every name." "Captain of our salvation." "Head over all things to His Church." Scattering His glorious gifts.

(Read Psalms lxviii. 18). "Ascended on high, received gifts for men; yea, even for the rebellious."

What gifts? (1) The gift of salvation for every poor sinner who comes unto God through Him. (2) The gift of Immortality, and the assurance of it through seeing Him rise from the dead and ascend into heaven. (3) The gift of His eternal Presence. Seems a strange thing to say when He was going away. Yet true. His presence no longer confined to one place at one time. He was again to be Omnipresent, pervading all creation. Illustrate—lamp on ground in a crowd only gives light to a few. When lifted up high it shines on all. (4) The gift of the Holy Ghost. (See Acts ii. 33). "He hath shed forth this." For some mysterious reason while He was here in bodily form, the Holy Ghost could not come. "But if I depart, I will send Him unto you." See the startling difference. The first sermon after Pentecost made more converts than the Lord's whole life on earth. A marvellous electrical power was over all. Who sent Holy Ghost, the Comforter, to put life into the Church, to rouse good thoughts, to help us towards God?

> "Whose gentle voice we hear,
> Soft as the breath of even;
> That checks each fault, that calms each fear,
> And speaks of heaven."

What great festival celebrates the coming of Holy Ghost? When will it be? We think of that in next lesson. We have been trying to sympathise with our Lord in His sufferings for us, in the glory of His self-sacrifice. Now let us sympathise with Him in His victory and His joy.

Let us lift up our hearts to Him gratefully to the heaven where He is gone, and pray that we may in heart and mind thither ascend, and with Him continually dwell (Collect for Ascension Day).

QUESTIONS FOR LESSON XXIII

1. Why should we feel sure there must be the Ascension?

2. In one verse the Lord states this? (John xvii. 28).

3. What was His last command to His church?

4. What was His attitude as He departed?

5. Tell of some of the gifts He left for men?

6. What was the angel's promise at the Ascension?

LESSON XXIV

THE COMING OF THE HOLY GHOST

St. John XIV. 14-26; Acts II. 1-16.

Teacher should strongly emphasise the difference this made—the Power that is now at our disposal. So many Christian people seem to forget this wonderful real power that is here for our help. God dwelling in us.

§ 1. Whitsunday

We have finished the story of our Lord's life on earth. We touch here for a moment His life after He left earth. He ascended into Heaven "to receive gifts for men." And the greatest of all these gifts which He sent down to us we think of to-day, THE COMING OF THE HOLY SPIRIT.

On what church holiday do we commemorate this? Whitsunday. Why so called? You would easily understand if you lived in the early days, 1600 years ago, when Whitsunday was especially the "White Sunday." It was one of the great baptismal seasons of the year, in memory of that day on which the Apostles had been baptised with the Holy Ghost. Christians met together on the "White Sunday" to receive into the congregation of Christ's Church those who had been admitted by Holy Baptism. In robes of pure white they entered the church, in token of the purity of life which Baptism denoted, while the chants of praise rose from the congregations for the white-robed throngs of spiritual children who in Baptism had been "born of water and the Spirit."

From very earliest times, even, it is said, from the days of the Apostles, the Church has kept this festival of Whitsuntide to commemorate—what? Yes, the most important event, perhaps, in the whole history of the world. Want you to understand to-day how important, and *what an enormous difference the fact of Pentecost made.*

Get clearly into your minds the gradual manifestation of God in the Bible. (1) In the Old Testament they knew of God in heaven who made all things and cared for men. (2) God came to earth in human form as Jesus Christ to show what the loving God was like and to live and die for men. (3) Then God came as the Holy Spirit to dwell not outside us but within us, caring for us, prompting us to do right and giving us power to do it. Now repeat these three stages for me.

§ 2. Our Lord's Promise

We have now come to the third stage in God's great plan for us. First see a prophecy before Christ came (Acts ii. 16-18). Then turn to what our Lord says (John

xiv. 16-18 and 25-27). What does He say in promising
that Holy Ghost should come? How long should He stay
with them? Should He be visible in human form like our
Saviour? (*v.* 17). "Shall be in you." What should He do
for them? (*v.* 26). Did anybody else in New Testament
prophesy of Holy Ghost? (Matthew iii. 11). Did anybody
in Old Testament? (Acts ii. 16-18). Did our Lord repeat
promise of Holy Ghost after Resurrection? (Acts i. 8).
What specially promised there as result of His coming?
Yes. Power was the great need of these few weak, simple,
ignorant Christians, who were to conquer the world for
Christ. Power was the great need of all the converts who
were to be members of Christ's "Kingdom of God."

§ 3. *The Story of Pentecost*

(Acts ii.) So after the Ascension the disciples waited
in Jerusalem for this great coming that was promised, as
our Lord commanded. They were wondering and excited
and puzzled. I don't suppose they quite understood. But
they were so accustomed to great wonders now that
nothing could much astonish them. Yet this must be
something very astonishing. God coming to them to
dwell with them and teach them and bless them and
give them power! What could it mean?

Picture the group in that room, meeting day after
day for earnest prayer and waiting. How solemn life
would seem! How real would be Christ and religion!
Day after day they meet, waiting, wondering, expecting
they scarce know what.

Then, at last, one of the great Church holidays

of the Jews. Which? Enormous crowds of Jews from all neighbouring countries crowded into Jerusalem. Whence? (*vv.* 9-11). The 120 disciples make their way through the crowds early (*v.* 15). Their morning prayer has begun. See them waiting, wondering, praying. Suddenly a most startling thing—the house shaking and quivering, as with earthquake, and they *hear*—what? And *see*—what? And *feel*—what? (*v.* 4). This last was the most wonderful of all—the shaking house and stormy sound and tongues of fire were as nothing to the great wonder of all which they felt in their own souls. Surely this must be the promised gift—this must be the Holy Ghost—God coming in mysterious power to equip the new Church for its work in the world! And then they discovered another wonderful thing that astonished everybody who heard. What? (*v.* 4). People came crowding together to inquire about the sound, as of a mighty wind, and as they crowd around, the disciples began to speak in the various languages of all the strangers. The Jerusalem people don't understand— it seems mere gabble. What do they think? (*v.* 13). But the strangers know better. Utterly astonished. What do they say? (*vv.* 7-11). Yes, it seems really the foreign tongues taught by miracle in a moment. Some think it was to enable them to go and preach to all these nations. I don't know. It seems a sort of prophecy of what the Church should do in the days to come. To-day the Church sends out missionaries to teach many peoples in their own tongue wherein they were born. The Bible Society sends out Bibles in 250 different languages through the world.

What did Peter reply to the mockers? Not filled with wine, but filled with what? (*v.* 4). Not the excitement of drunkenness, but the glorious enthusiasm for God and righteousness. Some cold, worldly people nowadays don't believe in this wonderful enthusiasm. Is it possible still? Yes; there are people now also very enthusiastic for God, willing to do and say and suffer anything if only they can carry out our Lord's blessed design for the Kingdom of God. But there should be far more people and far more power and enthusiasm. What would accomplish this? More of the power of the Holy Ghost? Now get it?

§ 4. *The Power of the Holy Ghost*

So this astonishing new power and light and strength came to these poor disciples and ever since comes to every poor weak disciple of Jesus who seeks it. Think of the wonder of it! God come into their hearts!

Now let us try to understand about the Holy Ghost. Just remember that this is God. Can we see Him? Feel Him? How? By His promptings within He speaks through conscience. Makes you feel His blame or praise. If you struck your mother, how should you feel? If you gave up something very pleasant to you for the sake of a sick comrade, how should you feel? That is the Holy Spirit's way of blaming and approving. Think how solemn! God really within us, rejoicing at every good deed, pained at every bad one. St. Paul expresses this finely and solemnly. "Your bodies are temples of the Holy Ghost." Do people all feel this blame and approval?

Yes, cannot help it. Do all obey? No. Then He is pained. Why does He want us to do the right and good always? Because He loves us, wishes us well, grieves to see us do what makes us bad and wretched. How good of God to care so much for us. (See Ephesians iv. 30). Now you know meaning of grieving Him.

But is it enough merely to urge us to do right? No. We cannot always do it. We often try and fail, and only sometimes succeed. But God dwelling within us does more. What? (Acts i. 8). POWER. What sort of power? Power to be good, holy, full of enthusiastic self-sacrifice for God and for righteousness. Most important to believe in this *power*. This is what makes that Pentecost Day so important. A new power came into life—to be the gift of every disciple of Christ for ever, if he would but reach out for it and use it. No one now *need be conquered* by evil. Great loss that people don't believe more in the Holy Ghost. Illustrate. Great power of electricity in the world always.

But men did not know. So they laboured and struggled and nearly killed horses drawing trams and could not send a rapid message, etc. Then new power discovered and all the world's work made easy. What a pity they did not know before. Or see a man in sore danger from robbers, and an army within hearing who would help him if he called out, or a weak man whose whole happiness depends on accomplishing a task too great for him, and help is near, but he does not know—does not believe it. Even many Christian people don't seem to realise yet this splendid power at their disposal through this great gift, the presence of the Holy Spirit.

What is the great distinction between Christianity and all other forms of religion? THIS POWER. Other teachers could tell men to try to do right. *Christ gives men power to do it.*

Even in Old Testament days the Church of God had not that power. A few men here and there got it by special inspiration; but it was not within the reach of all men, as now. They had cravings for good and efforts after right; but, compared with the great power of the Holy Ghost that Christ has given, their illumination and power was but

> "Like as moonlight unto sunlight,
> And as water unto wine."

See the power that came to these early Christians— the courage and self-sacrifice and enthusiasm about religion. In 100 years they had spread religion through the Roman Empire. Look at this sermon of St. Peter's, bearding priest and Pharisee and mob in Jerusalem itself, charging them with killing God's anointed (Acts ii. 23). Peter, who a few weeks before was afraid of a maidservant. See the effect of that great sermon of the Christian Church (Acts ii. 37-41). Why? Power of Holy Ghost. Look at what St. Paul, who received the gift long afterwards says of its effect on his own life and that of others. Read that passage about the fruits of the Spirit in a Christian's life. See what it does for him (Galatians v. 22, etc.) See what a power it is in the lives of the holiest, noblest people you know. (Emphasise this to make the Holy Ghost appear a *real* power whose effects they can see).

§ 5. Lessons

(1) *Believe in the Holy Spirit.* You will lose greatly if you do not. Your lives will be less strong, less happy, less beautiful. See how easy to get that gift. Jesus says, If ye poor evil people know how to give good gifts to your children how much more will the Heavenly Father give the Holy Spirit *to them that ask him.* He does not even say, "to them that trust Him or love Him." Just to them that ask. Is not that easy? Make it one of your regular daily prayers. "Thy Holy Spirit, O Lord, to me that ask Him."

(2) *Grieve not the Spirit* (Ephesians iv. 30). How could you do that? (a) By resisting His promptings. (b) By not using or caring for His help. He is the best friend you ever had. His great longing and craving is to make you holy and happy (Romans viii. 26). Yet so many disappoint Him. Think of a farmer looking on a field with which he had taken great pains and seeing poor, stunted growth—he turns away in sorrow. "Well, that field has disappointed me sadly!"

(3) *Quench not the Spirit* (1 Thessalonians iv. 19). Some even go so far as to quench His influence altogether. What an awful possibility! To push away the only hand that can lead us to Christ and to heaven. Pray: "O God, the Holy Ghost proceeding from the Father and the Son, have mercy upon us miserable sinners!"

QUESTIONS FOR LESSON XXIV

1. Meaning of name Whitsunday? Why?

2. Mention the three stages in God's manifesting Himself to men.

3. Mention any prophecies of the Holy Spirit in Old Testament and in the New.

4. Tell briefly the story of Pentecost.

5. Illustrate how men lose by not believing in the Holy Spirit.

6. State the three warning lessons.

LESSON XXV

THE HOLY TRINITY

Mark XII. 29. Hear, O Israel,
the Lord our God is One.

Matthew XXVIII. 19. Baptising into the name of
the Father and of the Son and of the Holy Ghost.

Some people tell me this lesson should be left out. Not that it is unimportant—it is most important—but that unthinking people and children cannot understand it. But we don't expect them to understand it fully. Nobody can. Yet if we leave it out see the danger of common notion—as if there were three gods. Also this lesson should help against the too free and familiar ideas of God as expressed in some popular hymns and teachings. We need to keep in mind the solemn majesty of God and preserve thoughts of awe and mystery side by side with thoughts of His tender love. The life of Christ is not complete without this lesson.

§ 1. *The Mystery of the Trinity*

We are to think to-day of a very difficult subject, the

210

mystery of the Holy Trinity. Think first why we have chosen these two verses to read. Why? (Let pupils find answers themselves.)

Trinity Sunday is the closing festival of the Christian year. Why is it necessary? We have been learning through these lessons of the *Father*, who sent the Son at Christmastide—of the chief events in the life and death of the *Son*—of the *Holy Ghost*, whose miraculous coming we thought of in last lesson. But foolish people might think that there were three Gods. So this festival celebrates the great fact of the Trinity. "These three are One." Meaning of Trinity? How could God be THREE and yet ONE? Can you understand? Why not? Because God is too great and high to be understood by such poor little creatures as we. Yet we may understand a little about the mystery.

Which is greater and higher in their nature, a stone or a fly? Which is greater and higher, a fly or a man? Which is greater and higher, man or God? Surely we might well expect that the infinite God who made and upholds all things would be of a nature higher and harder to understand than poor worms like us.

Let us invent a short fairy tale. A row of flies in a semicircle on window-pane—a big blue fly in the middle, like teacher in Sunday-school class. It is a Flies' Sunday-school. Very wise flies. Teacher is trying to explain the great and marvellous being, MAN, who is the owner of the house. This stupendous being consists of BODY, SOUL, and SPIRIT. He has an Intellect, a Conscience, a Will. He can talk to himself and answer himself back,

211

as if there were two beings in him. He feels remorse and enthusiasm, etc. Poor little flies try to understand till they are nearly black in the face. No use. "What is soul, spirit, intellect, conscience, remorse, enthusiasm?" "Are they things like the pane of glass we walk on, or like the sugar that we eat, or like the spider that we fear?" One very clever, pert young fly says, "I don't believe it, because I cannot understand it. No FLY is like that; so I don't believe a MAN is like that either." Do you think they could ever understand the higher nature of this being called MAN? Should you be surprised at their not understanding it?

Very much like our case. God is infinitely farther above us in His nature than we are above a fly. Should not be surprised if we can't understand when we are told of the mysterious nature of God. The fly on window-pane cannot understand the nature of man. And we can't understand the nature of God.

§ 2. Why We Believe It

Why do we believe in the Holy Trinity? Does the word occur in Scripture? No. But our Lord who of course teaches positively that God is One (*e.g.*, Mark. xii. 29) yet is continually talking of Father, Son, and Holy Ghost. Evidently He wanted us to know, *e.g.*, The Father sent me, "yet I and the Father are One." "The *Holy Ghost* whom *I* will send unto you from the *Father.*" Yet God is One. "Baptise into the name of Father, Son and Holy Ghost." Yet "Hear, O Israel, the Lord our God is One." I think God wanted us to know all we could about Him. If it did not matter, Jesus would not keep on repeating these things which made His teaching more difficult.

So we must not leave it out. Even though we can only hazily guess at its meaning we must believe it just because we trust our Lord who told us. I tell a blind man about the glorious sunset sky and the colours of the flowers. I tell a stone-deaf man about the delights of music. Does he understand? No. But because I tell him and he trusts me, he believes that some wonderful things called Light and Music exist, though he can never understand till he gets to another world. I think it is like that with us. Jesus evidently wanted us to know this wonderful thing about God. We can only say, It is certainly true, though like the little fly or like the blind and deaf man, my poor little mind cannot understand the wonders of the nature of God. That is all we mean in saying, We should believe in the Holy Trinity.

So we must believe in this mysterious fact, even though we can't understand the Trinity in Unity. The very fact of its difficulty is a confirmation of its truth, for surely no human writer of religion would have invented such a difficult doctrine. Story of St. Augustine trying to understand it as he walked on seashore. Little boy making a hole in the sand. "What for?" Looked up eagerly, and said, "Oh, I am going to scoop the sea into it." St. Augustine smiled at his simplicity, but said, "I am just as foolish, trying to put this infinite mystery of the Holy Trinity into my little mind."

§ 3. Why We Must Teach It

Foolish people say: Why not leave it out since it is so difficult?

The answer is: (1) Because it would be disrespectful to our Lord to leave out anything that He said so much about. He wanted us to know.

(2) Because it gives an idea of the greatness of God, the awe and mystery and wonder we should feel about Him who is so far away beyond us in His nature. Some people are inclined to be too free with God in popular hymns and popular notions, to think that the infinite God is someone perfectly simple and comprehensible like ourselves. It is only little people like ourselves that are so simple and easily understood. The more we learn of God the more He appears the wondrous, awesome, mysterious God that He must ever be—though with the tender, loving heart that makes Him so dear to us.

(3) Because of the danger of drifting into an utterly false notion as if there were three Gods—Father, Son and Holy Spirit. We are guarded from this by the doctrine of the Holy Trinity.

§ 4. The Love of the Blessed Trinity

Notice how your whole religious life is bound up with the Blessed Trinity. (1) What are directions about baptism into name of Trinity? (2) Repeat Gloria after Psalms. (3) Say the Benediction pronounced after church. (4) See Trinity in Te Deum. (5) In the Creed. The doctrine of Trinity is everywhere.

Let us not trouble to try to understand it. We cannot. Think practically about it. Hear the angels' songs in heaven (Revelations iv. 8). Though God is All-seeing—Almighty—All-present—yet this is not what the angels think about so much. Above all else is His holiness. His awful purity. Repeat the song?—Holy, Holy, Holy—three times repeated.

Think of the All-holy Father, of purer eyes than to behold iniquity, shrinking in horror and loathing from the touch of sin, devising a way that sinners should not be expelled from Him, and finding no way less awful than Calvary—so terrible is sin, so, holy is God.

Think of the All-holy Son come down to earth, so full of love for us that He bore our sins on the Cross.

Think of the All-holy Spirit proceeding from the Father and the Son, yet condescending to dwell in human hearts, entering at Baptism into the soul of a little child, struggling to keep hold of him in after life. Think what He says to every Baptised man, woman and child who has not utterly quenched the Divine life within him: "Your bodies are the temples of the Holy Ghost."

Think of God living in us as in a temple.

Think of the Holy Trinity—three Persons in one God—who took you into the Divine keeping when you were too young to keep yourself. Is it not touching—that love of God? When we bring a little child to Baptism, consign him, says Jesus, to the care of the Trinity; baptise him "into the name of the Father, the Son, and Holy Ghost." Think of that protecting love of God.

Though we cannot understand the mystery of the Trinity, we can think of it in this way—that God watches over our lives as a father watches over his erring boy—that God came down and took human flesh and suffered for us that we might be saved—that God is dwelling in us as the Holy Ghost, longing to make us pure and good. Thanks be to God!

QUESTIONS FOR LESSON XXV

1. Does the word Trinity occur in Bible?

2. Why then do we believe it?

3. Can we fully understand it? Why?

4. Give example of men believing in some degree what they do not understand.

5. What harm would come from omitting this doctrine?

6. State a way of thinking about it that we can understand. (See last paragraph of lesson.)

CPSIA information can be obtained
at www.ICGtesting.com
Printed in the USA
BVHW070323240519
549222BV00001B/66/P